D1202528

BOOKS BY WILLIAM J. JOHNSON

———

ROBERT E. LEE THE CHRISTIAN
GEORGE WASHINGTON THE CHRISTIAN
ABRAHAM LINCOLN THE CHRISTIAN

George Washington
the Christian

By
WILLIAM J. JOHNSON

mm mott media
BOX 236, MILFORD, MI. 48042

To the Memory of
Brison Blair and Lydia Overton Johnson
My Father and Mother
who taught their Children
from earliest childhood to
Revere the Name and
Emulate the Character
of
GEORGE WASHINGTON

In all thy ways acknowledge him, and he shall direct thy paths.—*Proverbs 3. 6.*

CONTENTS

ILLUSTRATIONS

THE REASON

My earliest recollection of the picture of the face of any man is that of the Father of his Country. The first and for many years the only pictures that hung on the wall of the old-fashioned sitting room in our southern Indiana home were those of George and Martha Washington. The story of the hatchet and cherry tree was one of the constructive influences in my life. As children we never tired of hearing stories of this great man.

Later, in school, as we studied the history of our country, and his part in it, he became to us a sort of demigod. Could a real man do what Washington did? He seemed to be the special care of Providence.

Afterward came the period of questioning. What made Washington great? What gave him his mighty power? What produced that incomparable character? Research disclosed that the supreme factor in his life was an unwavering faith in God and a strict adherence to his teachings.

Religion is the chief asset in any character. We cannot rightly estimate the character of any person until we know the religious belief of that person. Christianity is the basis of all true character and the foundation of all true greatness.

We have not tried to analyze the religious side of Washington's character, but to study its development and its expression. The chronological order has been followed, from birth to death. Our purpose is to place before the reader the evidence, and let him form his own conclusion. This evidence consists of what Washington himself said in his letters, diary, "orders" to the army, addresses and state papers, and authentic incidents in his life, gathered from many sources. Some things have been introduced which do not bear directly upon his religious belief or character, but they are interesting and suggestive sidelights.

Not finding any book which gave a complete and comprehensive study of the religious side of Washington's life, it seemed worth while to prepare such a work, that the young people of America may know the real secret of Washington's character and achievements. This is "The Reason" for adding one more book to the long list about Washington.

It is one hundred eighty-seven years since Washington was born in a humble Virginia pioneer's cabin, and one hundred twenty years since his body was laid in the tomb at Mount

Vernon.   All that can ever be known of him was written long ago.   The only thing that can be done now is to gather the facts in his life into such an arrangement as will most clearly exhibit to the student the true George Washington. This we have endeavored to do, so far as it relates to that matchless character which made possible such marvelous achievement.

The index numbers throughout the book will direct the reader to the sources of information under the heading "Where Found," in the back part of the book.   At the bottom of the page are given the date and the age of Washington at the time the incidents referred to on that page occurred.   All except the shorter quotations from Washington are in smaller type.

"The history of George Washington is not always a recital of brilliant exploits in the field— the cunning strategy of the commander; nor is it always a narrative of startling movements in the cabinet—the secret diplomacy of the Statesman; but it is *always* the consistent record of a man true to himself, true to his country, true to his God."

Merriam Park,
   Saint Paul, Minnesota,
   February 23, 1919.

W. J. Johnson

CHAPTER I

RELIGIOUS FOUNDATION

CHRISTIAN ANCESTRY

GEORGE WASHINGTON descended from a long line of excellent churchmen. His great-great-grandfather was the Rev. Lawrence Washington, a clergyman in the Church of England. His great-grandfather, John Washington, "a man of military talent and high in the government," came to America in 1657, settling in Virginia. He founded a parish which was named for him—"The parish of Washington." "He was also a sincerely pious man." In his will, he left a gift to the church, of "a tablet with the Ten Commandments," and recorded his faith in this manner: "being heartily sorry from the bottome of my hart for my sins past, most humbly desireing forgiveness of the same from the Almighty god (my saviour) and redeimer, in whom and by the meritts of Jesus Christ, I trust and believe assuredly to be saved, and to have full remission and forgiveness of all my sins."

His grandfather, also named Lawrence Washington, similarly expresses his faith in his will.

His father, Augustine Washington, was active in parish affairs, and became a vestryman in Truro Parish, Virginia, November 18, 1735, when his son George was three years old.

On the mother's side the line of churchmen is equally strong. Grandfather Ball was a vestryman, and Great-Grandfather Warner left his slender but excellent record by presenting to the parish church a set of silver for the holy communion. "The family of Balls was very active in promoting good things." Washington's uncle Joseph, in 1729, took the lead in a movement to educate young men for the ministry of the church. Mary Ball Washington (George's mother), says Henry Cabot Lodge, "was an imperious woman, of strong will, ruling her kingdom alone. Above all she was very dignified, very silent, and very sober-minded. That she was affectionate and loving cannot be doubted, for she retained to the last a profound hold upon the reverential devotion of her son."

If Washington's military character was developed out of materials which came to him by inheritance from both sides of his family, so too was his religious character. That love of the church which we have seen as a distinguishing mark in his family became a strong inheritance which his own will and intelligence did not set aside.[1]

17

Church Membership

The parents of Washington were members of the Church of England, which was almost the only denomination of Christians then known in Virginia.[2]

His Baptism

The birth record of Washington is found in an old family Bible of quarto form, dilapidated by use and age, and covered with Virginia striped cloth, which record is in the handwriting of the patriot's father, in these words:

George William, son to Augustine Washington, and Mary, his wife, was born the eleventh day of February, 1731-2, about ten in the morning, and was baptized the 3rd April following, Mr. Bromley Whiting, and Captain Christopher Brooks godfathers, and Mrs. Mildred Gregory godmother.[3]

According to the present style of reckoning, the birthday was February 22, and the baptismal day April 14.

His Father

There are many stories of Washington's boyhood which show that his father took great pains to teach George to be unselfish, inspire him with a love of truth, and teach him to know and worship God.

When George was eleven years old, his father died. Some months later he was sent to Westmoreland to live with his half-brother, Augustine, who occupied the family seat in that county. What the religious advantages were, which awaited him in his new situation, we have not the means to ascertain. There is no doubt that he enjoyed the privilege of public worship at the parish church, known then and now as Pope's Creek Church. Here his attendance was probably habitual, as it was an age in which everybody in that region frequented the house of God whenever service was performed.[4]

RELIGIOUS TEACHING BY HIS MOTHER

In addition to instruction in the Bible and Prayer Book, which were her daily companions, it was Mrs. Washington's custom to read some helpful books to her children at home, and in this way they received much valuable instruction. Among the volumes which she used for this purpose was one entitled Contemplations: Moral and Divine, by Sir Matthew Hale[5]—an old, well-worn copy, which still bears on its title-page the name of its owner, "Mary Washington." Those who are familiar with the character of Washington will be struck, on reading these "Contemplations," with the remarkable fact that the instructions contained in them are most admirably calculated to implant and foster such principles as he is known to have possessed.

The volume was found in the library at Mount Vernon, after Washington's death, and it appears to have been used by him through life.[6] There are many pencil marks in it noting choice passages.

"From that volume the mother of Washington undoubtedly drew, as from a living well of sweet water, many of the maxims which she instilled into the mind of her first-born."[7]

"Let those who wish to know the moral foundation of his character consult its pages."[8]

WASHINGTON'S RULES

In 1745, thirteen years old, Washington copied many things in a little book of thirty folio pages. One part was headed, "Rules of Civility and Decent Behavior in Company and Conversation." There were one hundred and ten of these maxims. "Scarcely one rule is there that does not involve self-restraint, modesty, habitual consideration of others, and, to a large extent, living for others."[9] The last three rules are as follows:

108th. When you speak of God or his Attributes, let it be Seriously & [with words of] Reverence, Honor & Obey your Natural Parents altho they be poor

109th. Let your Recreations be Manful not Sinful

110th. Labor to keep alive in your Breast that little Spark of Celestial fire called Conscience.[10]

RELIGIOUS FOUNDATION

POEM ON "CHRISTMAS DAY"

When Washington was thirteen years of age he copied some verses on "Christmas Day," beginning,

"Assist me, Muse divine, to sing the Morn,
On Which the Saviour of Mankind was born."[11]

Some think that he composed poems himself, but it is more likely that he copied them from an unknown source. It shows what manner of Christian training he had received at home. He had absorbed "the spirit of the Day and the facts of the faith, as well as the rule and model of Christian life."

GODFATHER

In 1747, at the age of fifteen years, young Washington was godfather to a child in baptism. In 1748, at sixteen, he was godfather to his niece, Frances Lewis. In 1751, at nineteen, to his nephew, Fielding Lewis, his sister's first child, and his mother was godmother. In 1760, at twenty-eight, he again became sponsor for another nephew, Charles Lewis.[12]

GOES TO MOUNT VERNON

In the summer of 1746, he finds his way to the home of his brother Lawrence, at Mount Vernon. From then until March, 1748, "George, it is believed, resided at Mount Vernon, and with his mother at her abode opposite to Fredericksburg. In that town he went to school, and as Mrs. Washington was connected with the church there, her son no doubt shared, under her own eye, the benefits of divine worship, and such religious instruction as mothers in that day were eminently accustomed to give their children. It was the habit to teach the young the first principles of religion according to the formularies of the church, to inculcate the fear of God, and strict observance of the moral virtues, such as truth, justice, charity, humility, modesty, temperance, chastity, and industry."[13]

TRIP TO THE WEST INDIES

In 1751 Lawrence Washington, on the advice of his physicians, decided to pass a winter in the West Indies, taking with him his favorite brother George as a companion. George kept a journal of this trip. They arrived on Saturday, November 3. The second Sunday we find this entry in his diary, which shows his habit of church attendance:

"Sunday, 11th—Dressed in order for Church but got to town too late. Dined at Major Clarke's with ye SeG. Went to Evening Service and return'd to our lodgings."[14]

Before the next Sunday he was stricken with smallpox. A few days after his recovery he sailed for home.

CHAPTER II

WASHINGTON'S PRAYERS

On April 21, 22, 23, 1891, there was sold at auction in Philadelphia a remarkable collection of Washington relics owned by Lawrence Washington, Bushrod C. Washington, Thomas B. Washington, and J. R. C. Lewis. Among them was found a little manuscript book entitled Daily Sacrifice.

"This gem is all in the handwriting of George Washington, when about twenty years old, and is, without exception, the most hallowed of all his writings. It is neatly written on twenty-four pages of a little book about the size of the ordinary pocket memorandum."[15]

"The occasional interlineations and emendations indicate that it was prepared for his own use."

Whether Washington composed the prayers himself or copied them from some source as yet unknown has not been determined; but they are a revelation of that striking character which has been the wonder of the world. Professor S. F. Upham, professor of practical theology in Drew Theological Seminary, wrote: "The 'Daily Prayers' of George Washington abound in earnest thought, expressed in simple, beautiful, fervent and evangelical language. They reveal to us the real life of the great patriot, and attest his piety. None can read those petitions, which bore his desires to God, and often brought answers of peace, without having a grander conception of Washington's character."

"The prayers are characterized by a deep consciousness of sin and by a need of forgiveness, and by a recognition of dependence upon the merits and mercies of our Lord. They contain fervent applications for family, friends, and rulers in church and state." The prayers are as follows (by special permission of Rev. Dr. W. Herbert Burk):

(1) SUNDAY MORNING

Almighty God, and most merciful father, who didst command the children of Israel to offer a daily sacrifice to thee, that thereby they might glorify and praise thee for thy protection both night and day; receive, O Lord, my morning sacrifice which I now offer up to thee; I yield thee humble and hearty thanks that thou has preserved me from the dangers of the night past, and brought me to the light of this day, and the comforts thereof, a day which is consecrated to thine own service and for thine own honor. Let my heart, therefore, Gracious God, be so affected with the glory and majesty of it, that I may not do mine own works, but wait on thee, and discharge those weighty duties thou requirest of me;

and since thou art a God of pure eyes, and wilt be sanctified in all who draw near unto thee, who doest not regard the sacrifice of fools, nor hear sinners who tread in thy courts, pardon, I beseech thee, my sins, remove them from thy presence, as far as the east is from the west, and accept of me for the merits of thy son Jesus Christ, that when I come into thy temple, and compass thine altar, my prayers may come before thee as incense; and as thou wouldst hear me calling upon thee in my prayers, so give me grace to hear thee calling on me in thy word, that it may be wisdom, righteousness, reconciliation and peace to the saving of my soul in the day of the Lord Jesus. Grant that I may hear it with reverence, receive it with meekness, mingle it with faith, and that it may accomplish in me, Gracious God, the good work for which thou has sent it. Bless my family, kindred, friends and country, be our God & guide this day and for ever for his sake, who lay down in the Grave and arose again for us, Jesus Christ our Lord, Amen.

(2) SUNDAY EVENING

O most Glorious God, in Jesus Christ my merciful and loving father, I acknowledge and confess my guilt, in the weak and imperfect performance of the duties of this day. I have called on thee for pardon and forgiveness of sins, but so coldly and carelessly, that my prayers are become my sin and stand in need of pardon. I have heard thy holy word, but with such deadness of spirit that I have been an unprofitable and forgetful hearer, so that, O Lord, tho'

I have done thy work, yet it hath been so negligently that I may rather expect a curse than a blessing from thee. But, O God, who art rich in mercy and plenteous in redemption, mark not, I beseech thee, what I have done amiss; remember that I am but dust, and remit my transgressions, negligences & ignorances, and cover them all with the absolute obedience of thy dear Son, that those sacrifices which I have offered may be accepted by thee, in and for the sacrifice of Jesus Christ offered upon the cross for me; for his sake, ease me of the burden of my sins, and give me grace that by the call of the Gospel I may rise from the slumber of sin into the newness of life. Let me live according to those holy rules which thou hast this day prescribed in thy holy word; make me to know what is acceptable in thy sight, and therein to delight, open the eyes of my understanding, and help me thoroughly to examine myself concerning my knowledge, faith and repentance, increase my faith, and direct me to the true object Jesus Christ the way, the truth and the life, bless, O Lord, all the people of this land, from the highest to the lowest, particularly those whom thou hast appointed to rule over us in church & state. continue thy goodness to me this night. These weak petitions I humbly implore thee to hear accept and ans. for the sake of thy Dear Son Jesus Christ our Lord, Amen.

(3) MONDAY MORNING

O eternal and everlasting God, I presume to present myself this morning before thy Divine majesty, beseeching thee to accept of my humble and hearty thanks, that it hath pleased thy great goodness to keep and preserve me the night past from all the dangers poor mortals are subject to, and has given me sweet and pleasant sleep, whereby I find my body refreshed and comforted for performing the duties of this day, in which I beseech thee to defend me from all perils of body and soul. Direct my thoughts, words and work, wash away my sins in the immaculate blood of the lamb, and purge my heart by thy holy spirit, from the dross of my natural corruption, that I may with more freedom of mind and liberty of will serve thee, the ever lasting God, in righteousness and holiness this day, and all the days of my life. Increase my faith in the sweet promises of the gospel; give me repentance from dead works; pardon my wanderings, & direct my thoughts unto thyself, the God of my salvation; teach me how to live in thy fear, labor in thy service, and ever to run in the ways of thy commandments; make me always watchful over my heart, that neither the terrors of conscience, the loathing of holy duties, the love of sin, nor an unwillingness to depart this life, may cast me into a spiritual slumber, but daily frame me more & more into the likeness of thy son Jesus Christ, that living in thy fear, and dying in thy favor, I may in thy appointed time attain the resurrection of the just unto eternal life bless my family, friends & kindred unite us all in praising & glorifying thee in all our works begun, continued, and ended, when we

shall come to make our last account before thee
blessed saviour, who hath taught us thus to pray,
our Father, &c.

(4) MONDAY EVENING

Most Gracious Lord God, from whom proceedeth
every good and perfect gift, I offer to thy divine
majesty my unfeigned praise & thanksgiving for
all thy mercies towards me. Thou mad'st me at
first and hast ever since sustained the work of thy
own hand; thou gav'st thy Son to die for me; and
hast given me assurance of salvation, upon my
repentance and sincerely endeavoring to conform
my life to his holy precepts and example.   Thou art
pleased to lengthen out to me the time of repentance
and to move me to it by thy spirit and by thy word,
by thy mercies, and by thy judgments; out of a
deepness of thy mercies, and my own unworthiness,
I do appear before thee at this time; I have sinned and
done very wickedly, be merciful to me, O God, and
pardon me for Jesus Christ sake; instruct me in the
particulars of my duty, and suffer me not to be
tempted above what thou givest me strength to bear.
Take care, I pray thee of my affairs and more and
more direct me in thy truth, defend me from my
enemies, especially my spiritual ones.   Suffer me not
to be drawn from thee, by the blandishments of the
world, carnal desires, the cunning of the devil, or
deceitfulness of sin. work in me thy good will and
pleasure, and discharge my mind from all things that
are displeasing to thee, of all ill will and discontent,

wrath and bitterness, pride & vain conceit of myself,
and render me charitable, pure, holy, patient and
heavenly minded.   be with me at the hour of death;
dispose me for it, and deliver me from the slavish
fear of it, and make me willing and fit to die whenever thou shalt call me hence.   Bless our rulers in
church and state.   bless O Lord the whole race of
mankind, and let the world be filled with the knowledge of Thee and thy son Jesus Christ.   Pity the
sick, the poor, the weak, the needy, the widows and
fatherless, and all that morn or are broken in heart,
and be merciful to them according to their several
necessities.   bless my friends and grant me grace
to forgive my enemies as heartily as I desire forgiveness of Thee my heavenly Father.   I beseech thee to
defend me this night from all evil, and do more for
me than I can think or ask, for Jesus Christ sake, in
whose most holy name & words, I continue to pray,
Our Father, &c.

(5)   TUESDAY MORNING

O Lord our God, most mighty and merciful father,
I thine unworthy creature and servant, do once more
approach thy presence.   Though not worthy to appear before thee, because of my natural corruptions,
and the many sins and transgressions which I have
committed against thy divine majesty; yet I beseech
thee, for the sake of him in whom thou art well
pleased, the Lord Jesus Christ, to admit me to render
thee deserved thanks and praises for thy manifold
mercies extended toward me, for the quiet rest &

repose of the past night, for food, raiment, health,
peace, liberty, and the hopes of a better life through
the merits of thy dear son's bitter passion. and
O kind father continue thy mercy and favor to me
this day, and ever hereafter; prosper all my lawful
undertakings; let me have all my directions from thy
holy spirit, and success from thy bountiful hand.
Let the bright beams of thy light so shine into my
heart, and enlighten my mind in understanding thy
blessed word, that I may be enabled to perform thy
will in all things, and effectually resist all tempta-
tions of the world, the flesh and the devil. preserve
and defend our rulers in church & state. bless the
people of this land, be a father to the fatherless, a
comforter to the comfortless, a deliverer to the cap-
tives, and a physician to the sick. let thy blessings
be upon our friends, kindred and families. Be our
guide this day and forever through J. C. in whose
blessed form of prayer I conclude my weak petitions
—Our Father, &c.

(6) TUESDAY EVENING

Most gracious God and heavenly father, we cannot cease, but must cry unto thee for mercy, because
my sins cry against me for justice. How shall I
address myself unto thee, I must with the publican
stand and admire at thy great goodness, tender
mercy, and long suffering towards me, in that thou
hast kept me the past day from being consumed and
brought to nought. O Lord, what is man, or the
son of man, that thou regardest him; the more days

pass over my head, the more sins and iniquities I heap up against thee. If I should cast up the account of my good deeds done this day, how few and small would they be; but if I should reckon my miscarriages, surely they would be many and great. O, blessed Father, let thy son's blood wash me from all impurities, and cleanse me from the stains of sin that are upon me. Give me grace to lay hold upon his merits; that they may be my reconciliation and atonement unto thee,—That I may know my sins are forgiven by his death & passion. embrace me in the arms of thy mercy; vouchsafe to receive me unto the bosom of thy love, shadow me with thy wings, that I may safely rest under thy protection this night; and so into thy hands I commend myself, both soul and body, in the name of thy son, J. C., beseeching Thee, when this life shall end, I may take my everlasting rest with thee in thy heavenly kingdom. bless all in authority over us, be merciful to all those afflicted with thy cross or calamity, bless all my friends, forgive my enemies and accept my thanksgiving this evening for all the mercies and favors afforded me; hear and graciously answer these my requests, and whatever else thou see'st needful grant us, for the sake of Jesus Christ in whose blessed name and words I continue to pray, Our Father, &c.

(7) A Prayer for Wednesday Morning

Almighty and eternal Lord God, the great creator of heaven & earth, and the God and Father of our

Lord Jesus Christ; look down from heaven, in pity
and compassion upon me thy servant, who humbly
prostrate myself before thee, sensible of thy mercy
and my own misery; there is an infinite distance
between thy glorious majesty and me, thy poor
creature, the work of thy hand, between thy infinite
power, and my weakness, thy wisdom, and my folly,
thy eternal Being, and my mortal frame, but, O
Lord, I have set myself at a greater distance from
thee by my sin and wickedness, and humbly acknowledge the corruption of my nature and the
many rebellions of my life. I have sinned against
heaven and before thee, in thought, word & deed; I
have contemned thy majesty and holy laws. I have
likewise sinned by omitting what I ought to have
done, and committing what I ought not. I have
rebelled against light, despised thy mercies and judgments, and broken my vows and promises; I have
neglected the means of Grace, and opportunities of
becoming better; my iniquities are multiplied, and
my sins are very great. I confess them, O Lord,
with shame and sorrow, detestation and loathing,
and desire to be vile in my own eyes, as I have
rendered myself vile in thine. I humbly beseech
thee to be merciful to me in the free pardon of my
sins, for the sake of thy dear Son, my only saviour,
J. C., who came not to call the righteous, but sinners
to repentance; be pleased to renew my nature and
write thy laws upon my heart, and help me to live,
righteously, soberly and godly in this evil world;
make me humble, meek, patient and contented, and

work in me the grace of thy holy spirit. prepare me for death and judgment, and let the thoughts thereof awaken me to a greater care and study to approve myself unto thee in well doing. bless our rulers in church & state. Help all in affliction or adversity—give them patience and a sanctified use of their affliction, and in thy good time deliverance from them; forgive my enemies, take me unto thy protection this day, keep me in perfect peace, which I ask in the name & for the sake of Jesus. Amen.

(8) WEDNESDAY EVENING

Holy and eternal Lord God who art the King of heaven, and the watchman of Israel, that never slumberest or sleepest, what shall we render unto thee for all thy benefits; because thou hast inclined thine ears unto me, therefore will I call on thee as long as I live, from the rising of the sun to the going down of the same let thy name be praised. among the infinite riches of thy mercy towards me, I desire to render thanks & praise for thy merciful preservation of me this day, as well as all the days of my life; and for the many other blessings & mercies spiritual & temporal which thou hast bestowed on me, contrary to my deserving. All these thy mercies call on me to be thankful and my infirmities & wants call for a continuance of thy tender mercies; cleanse my soul, O Lord, I beseech thee, from whatever is offensive to thee, and hurtful to me, and give me what is convenient for me. watch over me this night, and give me comfortable and sweet sleep to fit me for the service of the day following. Let my soul watch for the coming of the Lord Jesus; let my bed put me in mind of my grave, and my rising from there of my last resurrection; O heavenly Father, so frame this heart of mine, that I may ever delight to live according to thy will and command, in holiness and righteousness before thee all the days of my life. Let me remember, O Lord, the time will come when the trumpet shall sound, and the dead shall arise and stand before the judgment seat, and give an account of whatever they have done in the body, and let me so prepare my soul, that I may do it with joy and not with grief. bless the rulers and people of this and forget not those who are under any affliction or oppression. Let thy favor be extended to all my relations friends and all others who I ought to remember in my prayer and hear me I beseech thee for the sake of my dear redeemer in whose most holy words, I farther pray, Our Father, &c.

(9) Thursday Morning

Most gracious Lord God, whose dwelling is in the highest heavens, and yet beholdest the lowly and humble upon earth, I blush and am ashamed to lift up my eyes to thy dwelling place, because I have sinned against thee; look down, I beseech thee upon me thy unworthy servant who prostrate myself at the footstool of thy mercy, confessing my own guiltiness, and begging pardon for my sins; what couldst thou have done Lord more for me, or what could I have done more against thee? Thou didst send me thy Son to take our nature upon

"Note: The manuscript ended at this place, the close of a page. Whether the other pages were lost or the prayers were never completed, has not been determined."[16]

CHAPTER III

A CHRISTIAN SOLDIER

His Mother Advises Secret Prayer

In November, 1753, then twenty-one years of age, Washington was commissioned by Governor Dinwiddie, of Virginia, to be the bearer of dispatches to the French commander St. Pierre. He called to see his mother and explained the nature of his mission. "With her farewell kiss she bade him 'remember that God only is our sure trust. To Him I commend you.' "[17]

As he left the paternal roof, his mother's parting charge was, "My son, neglect not the duty of secret prayer." Never did a mother give better advice to her son, and never did a son more conscientiously follow it.[18]

"His uniform practice from youth to hoary age, furnished, it would seem, a consistent exemplification of this duty in its double aspect of public and private prayer."

Prayers at Fort Necessity

The first decisive indication of his principles on this subject, with which we are acquainted, appeared during the encampment at the Great

Meadows, in the year 1754. While occupying Fort Necessity it was his practice to have the troops assembled for public worship. This we learn from the following note, by the publisher of his writings: "While Washington was encamped at the Great Meadows, Mr. Fairfax wrote to him: 'I will not doubt your having public prayers in the camp, especially when the Indian families are your guests, that they, seeing your plain manner of worship, may have their curiosity excited to be informed why we do not use the ceremonies of the French, which being well explained to their understandings, will more and more dispose them to receive our baptism, and unite in strict bonds of cordial friendship.' It may be added that it was Washington's custom to have prayers in the camp while he was at Fort Necessity."[19]

Here we are informed not only of the pious custom of the youthful cammander, at the time and place mentioned, but are enabled to gather from the communication of Mr. Fairfax much that was highly favorable to the character of his young friend. Mr. Fairfax says, "I will not doubt your having public prayers in the camp." Intimate as this gentleman was with Washington, he would scarcely have so addressed him had he not felt encouraged to do so by his known sentiments of piety, if not his own habits. Mr.

Fairfax was the father-in-law of Lawrence Washington, the brother of George, and had possessed every opportunity of learning the character and conduct of the latter. Assured of his pious and serious deportment, he did not feel any hesitation in suggesting to him the expediency of the duty in question.[20]

"It certainly was not one of the least striking pictures presented in this wild campaign—the youthful commander, presiding with calm seriousness over a motley assemblage of half-equipped soldiery, leathern-clad hunters and woodsmen, and painted savages with their wives and children, and uniting them all in solemn devotion by his own example and demeanor."[21]

ACKNOWLEDGES AN ACT OF PROVIDENCE

In a letter to Governor Dinwiddie, dated Great Meadows, June 10, 1754, when twenty-two years of age, we have the following striking acknowledgment of a particular providential interposition in supplying with provisions the troops recently placed under his command:

We have been six days without flour, and there is none upon the road for our relief that we know of, though I have by repeated expresses given him timely notice. We have not provisions of any sort enough in camp to serve us two days. Once before we should have been four days without pro-

visions, if Providence had not sent a trader from the
Ohio to our relief, for whose flour I was obliged to
give twenty-one shillings and eight-pence per pound.[22]

His Custom to Attend Church

That it was customary with him to frequent
the house of God when in his power, appears
from the record made by him of an occurrence
among his soldiers, while encamped in Alexandria, Virginia, in the summer of 1754, having
himself returned but lately on a recruiting expedition from the Great Meadows: "Yesterday,
while we were at church, twenty-five of them collected, and were going off in the face of their
officers, but were stopped and imprisoned before the plot came to its height."[23]

His Trust in God

In April, 1755, the newly arrived General
Braddock offered him an important command.
His mother opposed his going to the war. In
the final discussion, the son said to his mother:
"The God to whom you commended me, madam,
when I set out upon a more perilous errand,
defended me from all harm, and I trust he will
do so now. Do not you?"[24]

Conducts Braddock's Funeral

General Braddock being mortally wounded in

the battle of the Monongahela, July 9, 1755, died on Sunday night, July 13. He was buried in his cloak the same night in the road, to elude the search of the Indians. The chaplain having been wounded, Washington, on the testimony of an old soldier, *read the funeral service* over his remains, by the light of a torch. Faithful to his commander while he lived, he would not suffer him to want the customary rites of religion when dead. Though the probable pursuit of savages threatened, yet did his humanity and sense of decency prevail, to gain for the fallen soldier the honor of Christian burial.[25]

LETTER TO HIS BROTHER

He wrote to his brother, John A. Washington, July 18, 1755, following Braddock's defeat, in which he says:

As I have heard, since my arrival at this place [Fort Cumberland], a circumstantial account of my death and dying speech, I take this early opportunity of contradicting the first, and of assuring you, that I have not as yet composed the latter. But, by the all-powerful dispensations of Providence, I have been protected beyond all human probability or expectation; for I had four bullets through my coat, and two horses shot under me, yet escaped unhurt, although death was leveling my companions on every side of me!"[26]

A CHRISTIAN SOLDIER

The Great Spirit Protects Him—
Testimony of Indian Chief

Fifteen years after this battle Washington and Dr. Craik, his intimate friend from his boyhood to his death, were traveling on an expedition to the western country, for the purpose of exploring wild lands. While near the junction of the Great Kanawha and Ohio Rivers a company of Indians came to them with an interpreter, at the head of whom was an aged and venerable chief. The council fire was kindled, when the chief addressed Washington through an interpreter to the following effect:

"I am a chief, and ruler over my tribes. My influence extends to the waters of the great lakes, and to the far blue mountains. I have traveled a long and weary path, that I might see the young warrior of the great battle. It was on the day when the white man's blood mixed with the streams of our forest, that I first beheld this chief. I called to my young men and said, mark yon tall and daring warrior? He is not of the red-coat tribe—he hath an Indian's wisdom, and his warriors fight as we do—himself is alone exposed. Quick, let your aim be certain, and he dies. Our rifles were leveled, rifles which, but for him, knew not how to miss—'twas all in vain, a power mightier far than we, shielded him from harm. He cannot die in battle. I am old, and soon shall be gathered to the great council fire of my fathers in the land of shades, but ere I go, there is something bids me speak in the voice of prophecy. Listen! *The Great Spirit protects that man, and guides his destinies—he will become the chief of nations, and a people yet unborn will hail him as the founder of a mighty empire.*"[27]

Discourages Gambling in the Army

In a letter to Governor Dinwiddie, from Alexandria, Virginia, February 2, 1756, regarding operations in the army, he says, "I have always, so far as was in my power, endeavored to discourage gambling in camp, and always shall while I have the honor to preside there."[28]

Intemperance and Profanity Discountenanced

The following letter to Governor Dinwiddie, written from Winchester, Virginia, April 18, 1756, shows his attitude toward intemperance and profanity:

It gave me infinite concern to find in yours by Governor Innes that any representations should inflame the Assembly against the Virginia regiment, or give cause to suspect the morality and good behavior of the officers. How far any of the individuals may have deserved such reflections, I will not take upon me to determine, but this I am certain of, and can call my conscience, and what, I suppose, will be still more demonstrative proof in the eyes of the world, my orders, to witness how much I have, both by threats and persuasive means, endeavored to discountenance gambling, drinking, swearing, and irregularities of every other kind; while I have, on the other hand, practised every artifice to inspire a laudable emulation in the officers for the service of their country, and to encourage the soldiers in the unerring exercise of their duty. How far I have failed in this desirable end I cannot pretend to say. But it is nevertheless a point which does, in my opinion, merit some scrutiny, before it meets with a final condemnation. Yet I will not undertake to vouch for the conduct of many of the officers, as I know there are some who have the seeds of idleness very strongly implanted in their natures; and I also know that the unhappy difference about the command which has kept me from Fort Cumberland, has consequently prevented me from enforcing the orders which I never failed to send.

However, if I continue in the service, I shall take care to act with a little more rigor than has hitherto been practised, since I find it so necessary.[29]

Intemperance Punished

His orders for preserving discipline must be allowed to have been sufficiently rigid. The following given in 1756 is a specimen:

Any commissioned officer, who stands by and sees

irregularities committed, and does not endeavor to quell them, shall be immediately put under arrest. Any non-commissioned officer present, who does not interpose, shall be immediately reduced, and receive corporal punishment.

Any soldier who shall presume to quarrel or fight shall receive five hundred lashes, without the benefit of a court-martial. The offender, upon complaint made, shall have strict justice done him. Any soldier found drunk shall receive one hundred lashes, without benefit of a court-martial.[30]

PROFANITY FORBIDDEN

In June, 1756, while at Fort Cumberland, he issued the following order:

Colonel Washington has observed that the men of his regiment are very profane and reprobate. He takes this opportunity to inform them of his great displeasure at such practices, and assures them, that, if they do not leave them off, they shall be severely punished. The officers are desired, if they hear any man swear, or make use of an oath or execration, to order the offender twenty-five lashes immediately, without a court-martial. For the second offense, he will be more severely punished.[31]

PROTECTION OF PROVIDENCE

From Winchester, Virginia, where he was stationed as commander of the troops, he writes to Governor Dinwiddie, about a year after Braddock's defeat:

A CHRISTIAN SOLDIER

With this small company of irregulars, with whom
order, regularity, circumspection, and vigilance were
matters of derision and contempt, we set out, and by
the protection of Providence, reached Augusta
Court House in seven days, without meeting the
enemy; otherwise we must have fallen a sacrifice
through the indiscretion of these whooping, hallooing,
gentlemen soldiers.[32]

CHAPLAIN FOR ARMY

While embarked in the French and Indian
War, as commander of the Virginia forces, he
earnestly sought of Governor Dinwiddie the
supply of a chaplain to his regiment. He writes
from Mount Vernon, Virginia, September 23,
1756, as follows: "The want of a chaplain, I
humbly conceive, reflects dishonor on the regiment, as all other officers are allowed. The
gentlemen of the corps are sensible of this, and
proposed to support one at their private expense.
But I think it would have a more graceful appearance were he appointed as others are."[33]

To this the Governor replied: "I have recommended to the commissary to get a chaplain, but
he cannot prevail with any person to accept of
it. I shall again press it to him."[34]

In answer to which Washington wrote, November 9, 1756: "As to a chaplain, if the government will grant a subsistence, we can readily
get a person of merit to accept the place, without

giving the commissary any trouble on that point."[35]

With this letter, of which this was part, the Governor seemed not to have been well pleased. In his reply, among other things, indicating displeasure, he says, November 24, 1756: "In regard to a chaplain, you should know that his qualifications and the Bishop's letter of license should be produced to the commissary and myself; but this person is also nameless."[36]

Washington answered, Nov. 24, 1756: "When I spoke of a chaplain, it was in answer to yours. I had no person in view, though many have offered; and I only said if the country would provide subsistence, we could procure a chaplain, without thinking there was offense in expression."[37]

Notwithstanding the importunity of Washington, no chaplain was provided by the government. His solicitude on the subject continuing at the recall of Dinwiddie, he wrote to the president of the Council from Fort Loudoun, April 17, 1758, as follows: "The last Assembly, in their Supply Bill, provided for a chaplain to our regiment. On this subject I had often without any success applied to Governor Dinwiddie. I now flatter myself, that your honor will be pleased to appoint a sober, serious man for this duty. Common decency, Sir, in a camp calls for the services of a divine, which ought not to be dispensed with, although the world should be so uncharitable as to think us void of religion, and incapable of good instructions."[38]

Conducts Religious Service in the Army

"I have often been informed," says the Rev. Mason L. Weems, "by Colonel B. Temple, of King William County, Virginia, who was one of his aides in the French and Indian War, that he has 'frequently known Washington, on the Sabbath, read the Scriptures and pray with his regiment, in the absence of the chaplain;' and also that, on sudden and unexpected visits to his marque, he has, 'more than once, found him on his knees at his devotions.'"[39]

Letter to His Fiancée

In the only known letter to Mrs. Martha Custis, to whom he was engaged, written from Fort Cumberland, July 20, 1758, he recognizes an all-powerful Providence:

We have begun our march for the Ohio. A courier is starting for Williamsburg, and I embrace the opportunity to send a few lines to one whose life is now inseparable from mine. Since that happy hour when we made our pledges to each other, my thoughts have been continually going to you as to another Self. That an All-powerful Providence may keep us both in safety is the prayer of your ever faithful and ever affectionate Friend.[40]

CHAPTER IV

THE ACTIVE CHURCHMAN

MARRIAGE

HE was married January 6, 1759, just after
the battle of Fort Duquesne, to Mrs. Martha
Custis, by the Rev. David Mossom, rector of
Saint Peter's Episcopal Church, New Kent
County, Virginia. Immediately they took up
their residence at Mount Vernon, and became
very active in church affairs.

BUYS BIBLES AND PRAYER BOOKS FOR STEP-CHILDREN

When John Parke was eight years old, and his
sister Patsey six, their kind stepfather, writing
to London in October, 1761, for articles of clothing and other things for the two children, includes the following for Master John:

A small Bible neatly bound in Turkey, and John
Parke Custis wrote in gilt letters on the inside of the
cover.

A neat small Prayer Book bound as above, with
John Parke Custis as above.

And the following for Miss Patsey:

A neat, small Bible, bound in Turkey, and Martha Parke Custis wrote on the inside in gilt letters.

A small Prayer Book neat and in the same manner.[41]

A VESTRYMAN

From 1748 till 1759 there was little church-going for the young surveyor or soldier, but after his marriage and settling at Mount Vernon he was elected vestryman in the parish of Truro and from that election he was quite active in church affairs.

At the time of which we are speaking, "the Established," or Episcopal Church, predominated throughout the ancient "dominion" (Virginia), as it was termed; each county was divided into parishes, as in England, each with its church, its parsonage, and glebe. Truro Parish at that time contained three churches, namely, old Pohick, the old Falls, and an old church in Alexandria.

(1) *Elected and Qualified*

The old vestry book of Pohick Church has this entry: "At a Vestry held for Truro Parish, October 25, 1762, ordered, that George Washington, Esq. be chosen and appointed one of the Vestry-men of this Parish, in the room of William Peake, Gent. deceased."[42]

The court records show that "At a Court held for the County of Fairfax, 15th February,

1763—George Washington, Esq. took the oaths according to Law, repeated and subscribed the Test and subscribed to the Doctrine and Discipline of the Church of England in order to qualify him to act as a Vestryman of Truro Parish."

Thus in due form Washington protested his loyalty and his orthodoxy, and took his place as one of the "twelve most able and discreet men of the Parish," whom the old statutes required to form the vestry.[43]

Among the manuscripts in the library of the New York Historical Society is a leaf from the church record of Pohick. It contains the names of the first vestry, and a few others. The following is a copy from the original. The names were signed at different times, during the summer and autumn of 1765:

"I, A B, do declare that I will be conformable to the Doctrine and Discipline of the Church of England, as by law established.

"1765. *May 20th*—Thomas Withers Coffer, Thomas Ford, John Ford.

"*19th August*—Geo. Washington, Daniel M'Carty," etc.[44]

(2) *Vestry Meetings*

The vestry seems to have met statedly twice a year, and at other times as occasion demanded. The meetings were usually held at one of the churches, but occasionally at the house of one or another of the vestrymen; and sometimes they lasted two or three days. Attendance upon these meetings from Mount Vernon involved a ride, going and returning, of from fourteen to forty miles. The vestry records attest, however, the regularity with which Colonel Washington was present; and when it is remembered how frequently his public duties and private interests took him out of the county, one is readily convinced that he brought to the discharge of the duties of this office the same conscientious purpose and fidelity which marked his career in more conspicuous stations. In his diary, though kept irregularly during this period, there are frequent references to his attending vestry meetings, such as the following:

1768—July 16—Went by Muddy Hole and Dog Run to the vestry at Pohick Church—stayed there till after 3 o'clock and only four members coming, returned by Captain McCartys and dined there.

September 9—proceeded [from Alexandria] to the meeting of our Vestry at the new Church [Payne's] and lodged at Captain Edward Payne's.

Nov. 28—Went to the Vestry at Pohick Church.

1769—March 3—Went to the Vestry at Pohick Church and returned at 11 o'clock at night.

Sept. 23—Captain Posey called here in the morning and we went to a Vestry.

1772—June 5— Met the Vestry at our new Church [Payne's] and came home in the afternoon.

1774—Feb. 15—I went to a Vestry at the new Church [Payne's] and returned in the afternoon.

Until called to the North in the service of his country, Washington continued in active and untiring service as a vestryman, and nominally held the office during the Revolutionary War.[45]

Washington resigned from the Vestry in 1782, in a letter to Captain Daniel McCarty, Esq., also a member, after a continuous membership of twenty years.[46]

(3) A Church Warden

The Church wardens were generally the executive and accounting officers of the vestry, having oversight of the church buildings and making repairs, and being charged with the relief of the poor and binding out orphans and indigent children as apprentices, making careful provision for their moral training and a meager education. They had also to present to the court or grand jury persons guilty of Sabbath-breaking, of not attending church, or disturbing public worship, of drunkenness, profane swearing, and other more serious immoralities, and to receive the fines imposed in certain cases for the use of the parish. Church wardens were elected each year; and in Truro the more prominent or more willing vestrymen seem to have served in some sort of rotation. Washington held this office for three terms at least within ten years.[47]

(4) *Falls Church*

The Falls Church derived its name from one of the falls of the Potomac. Originally it belonged to Truro Parish, being served by the same rector and the same vestry, of which Washington was a member. Later it became a part of Fairfax Parish, in which was Christ Church, Alexandria.

The old Truro Parish Vestry book records a meeting of the vestry at the Falls Church on March 28, 1763, at which George Washington was present. At that meeting it was resolved to erect a new building at the same place. In Washington's diary for 1764 is entered a copy of an advertisement for "undertakers to build Falls Church," showing him to have been on its original building committee.[48]

(5) *Payne's Church*

The vestry records show that "At a Vestry held for Truro Parish, the 28th, 29th and 30th days of November, 1765," George Washington being present, it was decided to build a new church in the upper part of the parish.

"At a Vestry held for Truro Parish at Mr.

William Gardner's on the 3d and 4th days of February, 1766," the site was chosen and the contract let. George Washington was made chairman of the building committee. The church became known as Payne's Church, from the name of the builder. It is in Fairfax County.[49]

(6) *Pohick Church*

Before the Revolution, Washington's regular place of worship was Pohick Church, seven miles west of Mount Vernon, although sometimes he went to the Episcopal Church in Alexandria, Virginia, ten miles north, both being in the same parish.

Pohick Church derived its curious name from a small river near it. Mount Vernon was in Truro Parish, and when the old place of worship went to decay (1767) there was considerable excitement among the people as to the location of the new one. A meeting for settling the question was finally held, and after George Mason had made a very pathetic speech, calling upon those present not to desert the spot which had been made sacred by the bones of their ancestors, Washington arose, and drew from his pocket an accurate survey of the whole parish, in which were marked the site of the old church, and the proposed location of the new one, with the residence of each parishioner. Having spread out

the map, and briefly explained it, he expressed
the hope that they would not suffer their better
judgments to be overruled by their feelings, and
sat down. The silent argument of the map was
perfectly convincing and the new site was determined on.[50]

In the year 1769 the plans of the new building
were drawn up, it is said, by Washington.[51] He
was chairman of the building committee and
supervised its erection. "A large share of the
expense incurred in its erection was borne by
Washington himself."[52]

CHURCH ATTENDANCE

He attended at one or the other of these
(Pohick or Alexandria) with his family every
Sunday, except when the weather was too inclement, and in such cases he read the church
service in the parlor at home.

His demeanor in church was always reverential and devout. He bore his part in the response, and bowed his head at the mention of
the name of Jesus in the Creed. Mrs. Washington and himself were both communicants.
As soon as the Custis children were old enough
they were instructed in the Church Catechism.[53]

"Mrs. Washington knelt during the prayers;
he always stood, as was the custom at that
time."[54]

Public Worship

The Rev. Lee Massey was the rector of the parish (Pohick Church) at the time referred to. He was a highly respectable man and shared much of the esteem of Washington. In regard to the religious deportment of his distinguished friend, especially in the house of God, he was often heard to express himself in the following strain: "I never knew so constant an attendant on church as Washington. And his behavior in the house of God was ever so deeply reverential that it produced the happiest effects on my congregation, and greatly assisted me in my pulpit labors."[55]

Not Kept from Church by Company

"No company ever withheld him from church," says the Rev. Lee Massey. "I have often been at Mount Vernon on the Sabbath morning when his breakfast table was filled with guests, but to him they furnished no pretext for neglecting his God, and losing the satisfaction of setting a good example. For, instead of staying at home, out of false complaisance to them, he used constantly to invite them to accompany him."[56]

Extracts from Diary

The following extracts from his diary (1768)

covering a few months are evidence of his faithful attendance at church at home or abroad:

May 8th, Went to Church from Colonel Bassett's.
May 22nd, Went to Church at Nomini.
May 29th, church at St. Paul's.
June 5th, to church at Alexandria.
June 12th, at Pohick.
August, Nomini in Westmoreland.
November 15th, at Pohick.[57]

A COMMUNICANT

In 1835 the Rev. E. C. M'Guire, rector of the Episcopal church at Fredericksburg, Virginia, writes as follows:

Among the aged persons residing in the neighborhood of Mount Vernon, and the descendants of such others, as have recently gone down to the grave, there is but one opinion in regard to the fact of his having been a communicant in the Pohick Church, previous to the Revolutionary War. The writer himself had it from a respectable lady, that she had once heard her mother unqualifiedly declare that General Washington was a communicant in that church, in the vicinity of which she had her residence, and on the services of which she attended. A living granddaughter of the Rev. Lee Massey, rector of Mount Vernon Parish for some years after Washington's marriage, says her grandfather on a special occasion told her the same thing in answer to a particular inquiry on the subject.[58]

"He partook regularly of the communion until he entered the office of general in the American Army."[59]

It was the custom in the colonial churches to administer communion only at Christmas, Easter, and Whitsuntide, and it was not an uncommon practice for communicants to receive only once a year.

Was Not Confirmed

There was no bishop in this country, and consequently no administration of confirmation until after the Revolution. There were many unconfirmed communicants in the church in the colonial days. The first bishop for the colonies was the Rev. Dr. Samuel Seabury. He was consecrated at Aberdeen, Scotland, November 14, 1784. It was early in 1785 when he arrived in America. Washington was then fifty-three years old. Having been a communicant and active in church affairs all his life, he probably did not feel the necessity of being confirmed at his age. It is very likely that he did not relish having an English-ordanied bishop, for in his diary, October 10, 1785, among other things, he adds, "nor any desire to open correspondence with the *new* ordained bishop."[60]

Grace at Table

But it was not in the duties of public worship

alone that Washington was careful to bear his part. Probably few Christians have been more attentive to their private devotions, at all times, and in all circumstances. No matter how urgent the business which engaged his attention, he never forgot his daily dependence upon God, and that his favor must be sought in earnest prayer.

It may be properly added, as an evidence of his devotional habits, that he always said grace at table. On one occasion from the force of habit he performed this duty when a clergyman was present—an instance of indecorum quite unusual with him. Being told of the incivility, after the minister's departure, he expressed his regret at the oversight, but added, "The reverend gentleman will at least be assured that we are not entirely graceless at Mount Vernon."[61]

PEW IN EPISCOPAL CHURCH, ALEXANDRIA

The new parish of Fairfax was separated from Truro Parish June 7, 1765. It included Falls Church and the church at Alexandria, Virginia.[62] There is no evidence that Washington was a vestryman in this Parish, as has been stated by some writers. A former attempt had been made to establish Fairfax Parish, and he had been elected a vestryman, but the parish never was organized, nor did the vestry ever meet or qualify.[63]

A new building was erected in Alexandria. It was completed in 1773. On the day it was turned over to the vestry, February 27, 1773, additional funds being needed, Washington purchased for thirty-six pounds, 10 shillings, the pew then known as Number 5, the highest price paid.

The Washington pew is the only square pew left, the others having been cut down and divided. He attended this church frequently before the Revolution, and regularly after his retirement to Mount Vernon.[64]

Going to Church in the Family Coach

"To the churchgoers the great family coach of the Washingtons was a familiar sight. Made in England, it was both substantial and elegant, if somewhat heavy. Four horses were necessary to draw it, but when the Virginia roads were very bad six were used; and to each span of horses there were the liveried postillion riders."[65]

Prays at Bedside of Dying Stepdaughter

Mrs. Washington's only remaining daughter (Martha) died on the 19th of June, 1773, at the age of sixteen. She was naturally of a frail constitution, and had for many months been gradually fading away. The heat of summer seemed rapidly to develop the seeds of consumption which were lurking in her system, and when her affectionate stepfather, the only father she had ever known, returned home, after a short absence at Williamsburg on public duty, he was shocked to discover the change. The tender and doting mother, upon whose watchful care the prolonged illness of the feeble child had made large drafts, was nearly overwhelmed with grief, and Washington, falling on his knees at the bedside, with a passionate burst of tears, prayed aloud that the loved one might be spared.[66] "Upon the wings of that holy prayer her spirit ascended, and when he arose and looked upon her pale and placid face, death had set its seal there."

"The sweet, innocent girl," Washington wrote, "entered into a more happy and peaceful abode than she had met with in the afflicted path she had hitherto trod."[67]

FASTING

In the year 1774 Washington went to Williamsburg as a member of the house of burgesses. The horizon of our country was then becoming dark with clouds, portending the approach of war. In the month of May, a short time after the members had assembled, information was received of an act of Parliament for shutting up the port of Boston—to take effect on the first of June. (The purpose was to crush the little rebel town of Boston, because of the "Boston Tea Party.") The members being much excited by this hostile proceeding on the part of the British government, when they met on the 24th day of May, passed an order that the 1st day of June "should be set apart by that house as a day of fasting, humiliation, and prayer, devoutly to implore the divine interposition for averting the heavy calamity which threatened destruction to their civil rights, and the evils of civil war, and to give them one heart and one mind, firmly to oppose, by all just and proper means, every injury to American rights."

June the first being the day appointed, the following brief entry is found in a diary kept by Washington at that time:

"June 1st, Wednesday.—Went to church, and fasted all day,"[68] thus conforming not only to the spirit, but to the strict letter of the order.

"He always meant what he said, being of a simple nature, and when he fasted and prayed there was something ominously earnest about it, something that his excellency the Governor, who liked the Society of this agreeable man and wise counselor, would have done well to consider and draw conclusions from, which he probably did not heed at all. He might have reflected, as he undoubtedly failed to do, that when men

of the George Washington type fast and pray
on account of political misdoings, it is well for
their opponents to look to it carefully."[69]

Announces Decision to Fight

After service (at Alexandria) one Sunday
morning in the summer of 1774, surrounded by
the congregation, every one of whom he well
knew, Washington advocated withdrawing alle-
giance from King George, and stated that he
would fight to uphold the independence of the
colonies. No more solemn time or occasion
could have been chosen. With calmness, in a
spirit of prayerful deliberation, he announced
his momentous decision under the very shadow
of the church.[70]

Washington Kneels During Prayer

The first of September, 1774, Washington left
home for Philadelphia as a member from Virginia of the First Continental Congress about to
meet in that city. It met on the fifth. The
first two days were spent in organizing and
arranging preliminaries, when it was proposed
that the sessions should be opened with prayer.
The Rev. Jacob Duché, an Episcopal clergyman,
was invited to officiate. The first morning,
September 7, 1774, he read the thirty-fifth
psalm, which begins as follows:

"Plead my cause, O Lord, with them that strive with me: fight against them that fight against me.

"Take hold of shield and buckler, and stand up for mine help.

"Draw out also the spear, and stop the way against them that persecute me: say unto my soul, I am thy salvation."

After the Psalm, Mr. Duché offered the following prayer: "O Lord our Heavenly Father, high and mighty King of Kings and Lord of Lords, who dost from Thy throne behold all the dwellers on earth, and reignest with power supreme and uncontrolled over all kingdoms, empires and governments; look down in mercy we beseech Thee, on these American States, who have fled to Thee from the rod of the oppressor, and thrown themselves on Thy gracious protection, desiring to be henceforth dependent only on Thee; to Thee they have appealed for the righteousness of their cause; to Thee do they now look up for that countenance and support which Thou alone canst give; take them, therefore, Heavenly Father, under Thy nurturing care; give them wisdom in council, and valor in the field; defeat the malicious designs of our cruel adversaries, convince them of the unrighteousness of their cause; and if they still persist in their sanguinary purposes, O let the voice of Thine own unerring justice sounding in their hearts constrain them to drop the weapons of war from their unnerved hands in the day of battle. Be Thou present, O God of wisdom, and direct the councils of this honorable assembly; enable them to settle things on the best and surest foundation, that the scene of blood may be speedily closed, that order, harmony, and peace, may be effectually restored; and truth and justice, religion and piety, prevail and flourish amongst Thy people. Preserve the health of their bodies and the vigor of their minds; shower down on them and the millions they here represent, such temporal blessings as Thou seest expedient for them in this world and crown them with everlasting glory in the world to come. All this we ask in the name and through the merits of Jesus Christ, Thy Son, our Saviour. Amen."[71]

JOHN ADAMS'S LETTER

John Adams, in a letter to his wife on the day following, thus describes the scene:

"You must remember this was the morning after we heard the horrible rumor of the cannonade of Boston. I never saw a greater effect upon an audience. It seemed as if heaven had ordained that psalm to be read on that morning. After this Mr. Duché unexpectedly to everybody struck out into an extemporary prayer, which filled the bosom of every man present. Episcopalian as he is, Doctor Cooper himself never prayed with such fervor, such ardor, such earnestness and pathos, and in language so eloquent and sublime, for America, for the Congress, for the province of Massachusetts Bay, and especially the town of Boston. It had an excellent effect upon everybody here."[72]

"Washington was kneeling, and Henry, and Randolph, and Rutledge, and Lee, and Jay, and by their sides there stood, bowed in reverence, the Puritan patriots of New England."

ATTENDS PUBLIC WORSHIP

The following entries made in his diary, show him still mindful of the Sabbath day, and of the the duty of public worship. Being a stranger in the city, and lodging at a public house, there may not have been the regularity of attendance which usually distinguished him:

September 25th—Went to Quaker meeting in the forenoon, and to St. Peter's in the afternoon; dined at my lodgings.

October 2d—Went to church, and dined at the new tavern.

9th—Went to the Presbyterian meeting in the afternoon; dined at Bevan's.

16th—Went to Christ church in the morning; after

which rode to and dined at the Province Island;
supped at Byrn's.[73]

"He is Always Right"

Mrs. Washington ardently sympathized with
her husband in his patriotic measures. To a
kinswoman who deprecated what she called "his
folly" Mrs. Washington wrote in 1774: "Yes,
I foresee consequences—dark days, domestic
happiness suspended, social enjoyments aban-
doned, and eternal separations on earth possible.
But my mind is made up, my heart is in the
cause. George is right; he is always right. God
has promised to protect the righteous, and I
will trust Him."[74]

CHAPTER V

THE COMMANDER-IN-CHIEF TRUSTS IN GOD

"God on Our Side"

When General Washington was told that the British troops at Lexington, on the memorable 19th of April, 1775, had fired on and killed several of the Americans, he replied: *"I grieve for the death of my countrymen; but rejoice that the British are still determined to keep God on our side,"* alluding to that noble sentiment which he later so happily expressed, viz: *"The smiles of Heaven can never be expected on a nation that disregards the eternal rules of order and right, which Heaven itself has ordained."*[75]

Letters to His Wife

In a letter to his wife, on Sunday, June 18, 1775, from Philadelphia, he expresses his trust in God as follows: "I shall rely, therefore, confidently on that Providence, which has heretofore preserved and been bountiful to me, not doubting but that I shall return safe to you in the fall."[76]

Just as he was leaving Philadelphia to take

command of the army, in another letter to his wife, June 22, 1775, he says: "I go, fully trusting in that Providence which has been more bountiful to me than I deserve, and in full confidence of a happy meeting with you in the fall."[77]

First General Order to the Army

July 4, 1775, the day after he took command of the army, an order was issued, in which we find the following injunction:

The General most earnestly requires and expects a due observance of those articles of war established for the government of the army, which forbid profane cursing, swearing, and drunkenness. And in like manner he requires and expects of all officers and soldiers, not engaged in actual duty, a punctual attendance on Divine service, to implore the blessing of Heaven upon the means used for our safety and defense.[78]

Prayers Every Morning

A few days after this order was published, the Rev. William Emerson, who was a minister at Concord at the time of the battle, and now a chaplain in the army, writes to a friend: "There is great overturning in the camp as to order and regularity. New lords, new laws. The Generals Washington and Lee are upon the lines every day. New orders from his Excellency are read to the respective regiments every morning, after prayers."[79]

ORDERS ARMY TO ATTEND DIVINE SERVICE

The Continental Congress having ordered a day of fasting and prayer, General Washington issued the following order, July 20, 1775:

The General orders this day to be religiously observed by the Forces under his Command, exactly in manner directed by the Continental Congress. It is therefore strictly enjoined on all Officers and Soldiers to attend Divine Service; and it is expected that all those who go to worship do take their Arms, Ammunition, and Accoutrements, & are prepared for immediate action if called upon.[80]

SUCCESS DEPENDS UPON ALL-WISE DISPOSER OF EVENTS

He sends a circular to the major and brigadier-generals, from the camp at Cambridge, September 8, 1775, asking their judgment of a proposed attack on the British at Boston, saying: "The success of such an enterprise depends, I well know, upon the All-Wise Disposer of events, and it is not within the reach of human wisdom to fortell the issue."[81]

RIGHTS OF CONSCIENCE

In his instructions to Benedict Arnold for

his campaign against Quebec, given at headquarters, Cambridge, Massachusetts, September 14, 1775, the last of fourteen items reads as
follows:

As the contempt of the religion of a country by
ridiculing any of its ceremonies, or affronting its
ministers or votaries, has ever been deeply resented,
you are to be particularly careful to restrain every
officer and soldier from such imprudence and folly,
and to punish every instance of it. On the other
hand, as far as lies in your power, you are to protect
and support the free exercise of the religion of the
country, and the undisturbed enjoyment of the
rights of conscience in religious matters, with your
utmost influence and authority.[82]

"RIGHTS OF CONSCIENCE"

In a letter to Colonel Benedict Arnold the
same day, September 14, 1775, he says:

I also give it in charge to you to avoid all disrespect of the religion of the country, and its ceremonies. Prudence, policy, and a true Christian
spirit will lead us to look with compassion upon their
errors without insulting them. While we are con-
tending for our own liberty, we should be very cautious not to violate the rights of conscience in others,
ever considering that God alone is the judge of the
hearts of men, and to Him only in this case they are
answerable.[83]

GEORGE WASHINGTON THE CHRISTIAN

Message to the Inhabitants of Canada

He sent a message to the inhabitants of Canada, which was printed in handbills before Arnold left Cambridge, with the view of having the copies distributed as soon as he should arrive in Canada. He says in part:

The Colonies, confiding in the justness of their cause, and the purity of their intentions, have reluctantly appealed to that Being in whose hands are all human events. He has hitherto smiled upon their virtuous efforts, the hand of tyranny has been arrested in its ravages, and the British arms, which have shone with so much splendor in every part of the globe, are now tarnished with disgrace and disappointment.[84]

Punishes Gambling

October 2, 1775, he issued the following order:

Any officer, non-commissioned officer, or soldier who shall hereafter be detected playing at toss-up, pitch, and hustle, or any other games of chance, in or near the camp or village bordering on the encampments, shall without delay be confined and punished for disobedience of orders. The General does not mean by the above to discourage sports of exercise or recreation, he only means to discountenance and punish gaming.[85]

Hospitality to the Poor

On Sunday, the 26th of November, 1775, the

General writes from Cambridge to Lund Washington, Mount Vernon, superintendent of his plantations and business agent during the Revolution, giving instructions thus:

Let the hospitality of the house, with respect to the poor, be kept up. Let no one go hungry away. If any of this kind of people should be in want of corn, supply their necessities, provided it does not encourage them in idleness, and I have no objection to your giving my money in charity to the amount of forty or fifty pounds a year when you think it well bestowed. What I mean by having no objection is that it is my desire that it should be done. You are to consider that neither myself nor wife is now in the way to do these good offices. In all other respects I recommend it to you, and have no doubt of your observing the greatest economy and frugality; as I suppose you know that I do not get a farthing for my services here, more than my expenses. It becomes necessary, therefore, for me to be saving at home.[86]

And while speaking on this subject, it will not be amiss to add, that one of the General's managers, Mr. Peake, a respectable man, after the war, once said in reference to this subject:

"I had orders from General Washington to fill a corn-house every year for the sole use of the poor in my neighborhood, to whom it was a most seasonable and precious relief, saving numbers of poor women and children from extreme want, and blessing with plenty.

"And when, on one occasion, much distress prevailed in the country round, on account of the failure of the harvest, he purchased several bushels of corn at a high price to be given away to those who were most in want, and most deserving of relief."[87]

His benevolence "was a quiet and unfailing stream, which never brawled its way in the noonday sun, but flowed silently and unseen, and only betrayed its course by the green fertility of its margin."[88]

Attends Church

On Sunday, December 3, 1775, he attended service at the Rev. Dr. Appleton's Church; discourse by Abiel Leonard, chaplain to General Putnam's command. This was the "Old Congregational Church," which Washington attended while in Cambridge, the minister being the venerable Nathaniel Appleton.[89]

The first Sunday after Mrs. Washington arrived at headquarters, Christ Church (Episcopal) being used for military purposes, they attended the Congregational church, as noted in Dorothy Dudley's diary, as follows:

"December 18th—Mrs. Washington was at

church yesterday with the General. . . . Dr.
Appleton prayed most earnestly for our country
and its defenders, alluding pointedly and affec-
tionately to the chief officer of the army. . . .
Mrs. Washington has expressed a wish that
Christ Church may be put in readiness for
services, and orders have gone forth to that
effect."[90]

Two weeks later service was held in Christ
Church as shown by the following interesting
note in the diary of Dorothy Dudley:

"January 1, 1776.—Yesterday service was
held in Christ Church. I was invited to be
present. Colonel William Palfrey, at request
of Mrs. Washington, read the service and made a
prayer of a form different from that commonly
used for the King. . . . General and Mrs. Washington, Mrs. Gates, Mrs. Morgan, Mrs. Mifflin,
Mrs. Curtis, and many others, including officers,
were present. The General is loyal to his
church as to his country, though he had identi-
fied himself with our parish [Congregational]
during his residence among us. . . . The General's majestic figure bent reverently in prayer
as with devout earnestness he entered into the
service."[91]

FINGER OF PROVIDENCE

He writes to Joseph Reed on Sunday, January

14, 1776, concerning difficulties of the army—
lack of food, clothing, guns, etc., as follows:

The reflection on my situation, and that of this
army, produce many an unhappy hour when all
around me are wrapped in sleep.   Few people know
the predicament we are in, on a thousand accounts;
fewer still will believe, if any disaster happens to
these lines, from what cause it flows.   I have often
thought how much happier I should have been, if,
instead of accepting the command under such circumstances, I had taken my musket on my shoulder
and entered the ranks, or, if I could have justified
the measure to posterity and my own conscience,
have retired to the back country and lived in a wig-
wam.   If I shall be able to rise superior to these and
many other difficulties which might be enumerated,
I shall most religiously believe that the finger of
Providence is in it, to blind the eyes of our enemies;
for surely if we get well through this month, it must
be for want of their knowing the disadvantages we
labor under.[92]

GAMBLING AGAIN CONDEMNED

On the 26th of February, 1776, the following
orders were issued:

All officers, non-commissioned officers, and soldiers
are positively forbid playing at cards and other
games of chance.   At this time of public distress
men may find enough to do in the service of their

God and their country, without abandoning themselves to vice and immorality.[93]

FAST DAY

March 6, 1776, General Washington issued at Cambridge the following order:

Thursday, the 7th instant, being set apart by the honorable the Legislature of this Province as a day of fasting, prayer, and humiliation, "to implore the Lord and Giver of all victory to pardon our manifold sins and wickedness, and that it would please Him to bless the Continental arms with His divine favor and protection," all officers and soldiers are strictly enjoined to pay all due reverence and attention on that day to the sacred duties to the Lord of hosts for His mercies already received, and for those blessings which our holiness and uprightness of life can alone encourage us to hope through His mercy to obtain.[94]

SPECIAL PROVIDENCE

In his answer to an address from the General Assembly of Massachusetts, following evacuation of Boston by the British, March 17, 1776, he closed:

And it being effected without the blood of our soldiers and fellow-citizens must be ascribed to the interposition of that Providence which has manifestly appeared in our behalf through the whole of this important struggle, as well as to the measures pursued for bringing about the happy event.

May that Being who is powerful to save, and in whose hands is the fate of nations, look down with an eye of tender pity and compassion upon the whole of the United Colonies; may He continue to smile upon their counsels and arms, and crown them with success, whilst employed in the cause of virtue and mankind. May this distressed colony and its capital, and every part of this wide extended continent, through His divine favor, be restored to more than their former lustre and once happy state, and have peace, liberty, and safety secured upon a solid, permanent, and lasting foundation.[95]

ATTENDS THANKSGIVING SERVICE

On the same day, a few hours after the departure of the British, Washington and his officers attended thanksgiving service, and listened to the Rev. Dr. Abiel Leonard preach from Exodus 14. 25: "And he took off their chariot wheels, that they drave them heavily; so that the Egyptians said, Let us flee from the face of Israel; for the Lord fighteth for them against the Egyptians."[96]

ASKS FOR THANKSGIVING SERMON

In his journal for March 23, 1776, Dr. James Thacher says that when Washington entered Boston after the evacuation by the British, "He [Washington] requested Reverend Doctor [Andrew] Eliot, at the renewal of his customary

Thursday lecture, to preach a thanksgiving sermon, adapted to the joyful occasion. Accordingly, on the 28th, this pious divine preached an appropriate discourse."[97]

THE THANKSGIVING SERVICE

A newspaper at the time gave the following account of the service:

Thursday [March 28] the Lecture, which was established, and has been observed from the first settlement of Boston, without interruption, until within these few months past, was opened by the Reverend Doctor Eliot. His Excellency General Washington, the other General Officers and their suites, having been previously invited, met in the Council Chamber, from whence, preceded by the Sheriff with his Wand, attended by the members of the Council, who had had the smallpox, the Committee of the House of Representatives, the Selectmen, the Clergy, and many other Gentlemen, they repaired to the old Brick Meeting House, where an excellent and well adapted discourse was delivered from those words in the XXXIII chapter of Isaiah, and 20th verse. After divine service was ended his Excellency, attended and accompanied as before, returned to the Council Chamber, from whence they proceeded to the Bunch of Grapes tavern, where an elegant dinner was provided at the public expense. . . . Joy and gratitude sat on every countenance, and smiled in every eye.[98]

Interposition of Providence

In a letter to his brother, John Augustine Washington, written from Cambridge, Massachusetts, March 31, 1776, speaking of the evacuation of Boston, he says:

Upon their discovery of the works next morning, great preparations were made for attacking them; but not being ready before the afternoon, and the weather getting very tempestuous, much blood was saved, and a very important blow, to one side or the other, was prevented. That this most remarkable interposition of Providence is for some wise purpose, I have not a doubt.[99]

No Kind of Amusements

Washington was very strict in his deportment in the army. Concerning horse-racing, gambling, etc., in a letter to the President of Congress, dated New York, April, 1776, he thus writes: "I give in to no kind of amusements myself and consequently those about me [alluding to his aids] can have none."[100]

Prayers for King to be Omitted

Soon after Washington assumed command in New York he sent word to Dr. Inglis, then assistant rector of the Trinity Church in that city, that he would be glad to have the prayers for the king and the royal family omitted. The

American general was sincerely desirous to be present at the services of his own church; but a person of even less ingrained veracity than General Washington would have scrupled to join in supplications for the victory of a monarch against whom he had set in line of battle twenty thousand soldiers, carrying pouches filled with bullets which had been cast from the metal of his Majesty's statue.[101]

OBSERVANCE OF A FAST

May 15, 1776, he issued the following order:

The Continental Congress having ordered Friday the 17th instant to be observed as a day of fasting, humiliation, and prayer, humbly to supplicate the mercy of Almighty God, that it would please Him to pardon all our manifold sins and transgressions, and to prosper the arms of the United Colonies, and finally establish the peace and freedom of America upon a solid and lasting foundation; the General commands all officers and soldiers to pay strict obedience to the orders of the Continental Congress; that, by their unfeigned and pious observance of their religious duties, they may incline the Lord and Giver of victory to prosper our arms.[102]

BELIEVES CAUSE JUST

In a letter to John Augustine Washington, written from Philadelphia, May 31, 1776, speaking of the army being unprepared for the bloody campaign which was evidently before it, he says, "However, it is to be hoped, that, if our cause is just, as I do most religiously believe it to be, the same Providence, which has in many instances appeared for us, will still go on to afford its aid."[103]

Relies upon Supreme Being

In view of an expected attack from the combined forces of the enemy, the following order was issued, July 2, 1776:

The time is now near at hand which must probably determine whether Americans are to be freemen or slaves; whether they are to have any property they can call their own; whether their houses and farms are to be pillaged and destroyed, and they consigned to a state of wretchedness, from which no human efforts will probably deliver them. The fate of unborn millions will now depend, under God, on the courage and conduct of this army. Our cruel and unrelenting enemy leaves us no choice but a brave resistance or the most abject submission. This is all that we can expect. We have, therefore, to resolve to conquer or die. Our own country's honor calls upon us for a vigorous and manly exertion, and if we now shamefully fail, we shall become infamous to the whole world. Let us rely upon the goodness of the cause, and the aid of the Supreme Being, in whose hands victory is, to animate and encourage us to great and noble actions, etc.[104]

TRUSTS IN GOD

"A Christian Soldier"

On July 9, 1776, General Washington issued the following order:

The honorable Continental Congress having been pleased to allow a chaplain to each regiment, with the pay of thirty-three dollars and one-third per month, the colonels or commanding officers of each regiment are directed to procure chaplains accordingly, persons of good characters and exemplary lives, and to see that all inferior officers and soldiers pay them a suitable respect. The blessing and protection of Heaven are at all times necessary, but especially so in times of public distress and danger. The General hopes and trusts, that every officer and man will endeavor so to live and act as becomes a Christian soldier, defending the dearest rights and liberties of his country.[105]

Profanity Condemned

August 3, 1776, he issued the following order:

That the troops may have an opportunity of attending public worship, as well as to take some rest after the great fatigue they have gone through, the General in future excuses them from fatigue duty on Sundays, except at shipyards, or on special occasions, until further orders. The General is sorry to be informed that the foolish and wicked practice of profane cursing and swearing, a vice heretofore little known in an American Army, is growing into fashion; he hopes the officers will by example as well as in-

fluence, endeavor to check it; and that both they and
the men will reflect that we can have little hope of
the blessing of Heaven on our arms if we insult it by
our impiety and folly; added to this, it is a vice so
mean and low, without any temptation, that every
man of sense and character detests and despises it.[106]

PRAYER BEFORE BATTLE

Just before the engagement on the battlefield
of Chatterton Hill, October 28, 1776, it is said
that in the home where he was entertained, he
wrestled in prayer with the God of battles.
"His loyal heart, stung with the epithet 'rebel'
hurled at patriots, was, at the family altar,
poured out into the language of the very 'Bible
hero without a flaw' he is said to resemble. His
words were those of the 22d verse of chapter 22
of the book of Joshua: 'The Lord, God of gods,
he knoweth, and Israel he shall know; if it be in
rebellion, or if in transgression against the
Lord.'"[107]

CHAPTER VI

WASHINGTON ATTENDS COMMUNION SERVICE

(1) ARMY ENCAMPED AT MORRISTOWN, NEW JERSEY

"During his sojourn at Morristown, New Jersey, in the winter of 1777, Washington had been severely tried. A scourge of smallpox, the prevalence of other fatal diseases, the privations and sufferings of the soldiers, frequent desertions and Washington himself seriously ill with quinsy sore throat, when his death seemed imminent— these were the causes of a depression of spirit on the part of the Commander-in-chief, which only appeal (as he came at last to realize) to a higher than merely human power could adequately relieve. To that higher power, Washington, like many before and since, turned in his extremity for support and consolation.

"It was, presumably, while experiencing the depression of spirit consequent upon the suggested multiplicity of difficulties confronting him, that the Commander-in-chief, one morning, after his accustomed daily inspection of camp at Lowantica Valley (now Spring Valley), called upon 'Parson Johnes' at his home. These two men were no strangers to each other; neither was this the initial visit to the Presbyterian parsonage of the Commander of the American army, encamped at the country seat of Morris. Association in the work of devising means and methods for the control of the smallpox and other diseases in the army and in the village; occasional, and perhaps frequent, attendance upon religious services conducted on Sunday by the beloved pastor of the only Presbyterian church then in Morristown; and association, also, in the important deliberations at the Presbyterian parsonage of the New Jersey Council of Safety, in which both Washington and Dr. Johnes had participated, had doubtless resulted in a mutual acquaintance of these two men, which had ripened into a friendship of no ordinary character."[108]

(2) Testimony of Reverend Samuel H. Coxe, D.D.

It was during this time that Washington partook of the communion. The story was first published in Dr. Hosack's Life of DeWitt Clinton in 1829, and related in the words of the Rev. Samuel H. Coxe, D.D. (pastor of Laight Street Presbyterian Church, New York city), and father of the late Bishop Coxe, of the Epis-

copal Church. Dr. Coxe received the account
from Dr. Hillyer, who had it directly from Dr.
Timothy Johnes:

"It was on a morning of a week previous to the
semiannual celebration of the Lord's Supper in
the Presbyterian church, that Washington drove
up to the home of Dr. Johnes. He left his hand-
some bay horse in charge of his mounted orderly,
and with stately but heavy tread, ascended the
steps of the front veranda and lifted the old-
fashioned brass knocker on the door, whose
short, ¹ distinct rap would gain him admission."[109]

"I have the following anecdote," says Dr.
Coxe, "from unquestionable authority. It has
never, I think, been given to the public; but I
received it from a venerable clergyman, who had
it from the lips of the Rev. Dr. Jones [Johnes]
himself. To all Christians, and to all Americans, it cannot fail to be acceptable:

"While the American army, under the command of Washington, lay encamped at Morristown, New Jersey [winter of 1776-7], it occurred
that the service of the communion [then observed semiannually only] was to be administered in the Presbyterian church of that village.
In a morning of the previous week the General,
after his accustomed inspection of the camp,

visited the house of the Rev. Doctor Jones [Johnes], then pastor of the church, and, after the usual preliminaries, thus accosted him:

" 'Doctor, I understand that the Lord's Supper is to be celebrated with you next Sunday. I would learn if it accords with the canon of your church to admit communicants of another denomination?'

"The Doctor rejoined, 'Most certainly; ours is not the Presbyterian table, General, but the Lord's table; and we hence give the Lord's invitation to all his followers, of whatever name.'

"The General replied, 'I am glad of it; that is as it ought to be; but, as I was not quite sure of the fact, I thought I would ascertain it from yourself, as I propose to join with you on that occasion. Though a member of the Church of England, I have no exclusive partialities.'

"The Doctor reassured him of a cordial welcome, and the General was found seated with the communicants the next Sabbath."[110]

This incident in the life of Washington shows his own impressions that he was a *religious man*, entitled to the privileges of the household of faith. The circumstance that makes it remarkable is, that it was the only time during the Revolutionary War that he is certainly known to have celebrated the sacrament of the Lord's Supper.

(3) REGULAR ATTENDANT AT CHURCH

"The pulpit of the Morristown Presbyterian Church was occupied by Doctor Timothy Johnes, whose contemporaries describe him as a mild but eminently persuasive preacher, and as a most admirable pastor. Washington was a constant attendant on his preaching, both winters he spent in Morristown."[111]

"That Washington and other American officers and soldiers occasionally attended open-air services, held in the orchard in the rear of the Presbyterian parsonage, is now too well authenticated to question."[112]

(4) SACRAMENT UNDER AN APPLE TREE

The Reverend E. C. M'Guire, an Episcopal clergyman of Fredericksburg, Virginia, in 1835, obtained some valuable information, which is given herewith. Mr. M'Guire married Judith, the daughter of Robert Lewis, Washington's nephew and agent, and for a time his private secretary, and had unusually good sources of information. It seems that the communion was held under an apple tree, and that Washington wrote the pastor a note instead of calling on him personally. Dr. M'Guire's statement follows:

"That he partook of the communion at Morristown, New Jersey, during the encampment of the army there, in 1780 [1777], has long been an accredited tradition. Some few, indeed, have been doubtful, but it would seem without any good ground. That the account as generally stated, is in the main correct, let the following communications attest. They were written in answer to letters requesting information on the point to which they refer. The high respectability of the writers will gain for their testimony the utmost confidence of those who know them."[113]

(5) TESTIMONY OF MR. ASA A. COULTON
MORRISTOWN, March 26, 1836.

REV. AND DEAR SIR,

Yours was duly received, and ought perhaps to have been sooner answered; but I have delayed a little hoping to make my statements the stronger by additional testimony.

I do not learn that any living witness to the fact in question can be found in this vicinity, though it is believed there are such. I have called on Mr. Wm. Johnes, a son of Reverend Doctor Johnes, to whom you refer. By reason of his great age, he can say nothing upon the subject, but Mrs. Johnes, who is much younger, gives it as an unquestioned family tradition, that General Washington wrote the note in question, and partook of the sacrament as it has been commonly reported. Mrs. Johnes refers directly to her father-in-law, the Reverend Doctor Johnes. The family are still in possession of the orchard, and point out the very tree under which the sacrament was then administered, the church being at that time occupied as a hospital. The fact in question is regarded as certain by the older residents of the place, beyond all room for doubt.

It is thought by some, that the Reverend Doctor Richards, of Auburn Theological Seminary, New York, is in possession of the very note, written by General Washington to Doctor Johnes, relative to his admission to the communion.

Respectfully, Sir, I am truly yours,

Asa S. Coulton.[114]

(6) Testimony of Rev. James Richards, D.D.

The following letter is from Dr. Richards, the gentleman referred to in the foregoing letter:

Auburn, 14th of April, 1836.

Dear Sir,

Yours of the 5th has just been received. I can only say in reply, that I never saw the note to which you allude,—but have no doubt that such a note was addressed by Washington to Doctor Johnes, of Morristown, on the occasion to which you refer. I became a resident in that town in the summer of 1794, while Doctor Johnes was still living—and was afterwards the regular pastor of that congregation for about fourteen years. The report that Washington did actually receive the communion from the hands of Doctor Johnes, was universally current during that period, and so far as I know, never contradicted. I have often heard it from the members of Doctor Johnes' family, while they added that a

GEORGE WASHINGTON THE CHRISTIAN

note was addressed by Washington to their father,
requesting the privilege, and stating that though connected with the Episcopal Church, he felt a freedom
and desire to commune with those of another name,
if acceptable to them. Very often, too, have I
heard this circumstance spoken of as evidence of
that great man's liberality, as well as piety.

There were hundreds at Morristown during the
time of which I speak, who might, if the fact of Washington's receiving the communion there be true,
have witnessed that fact—and who would not be
slow to contradict it, on the supposition that it had
not been witnessed by them or their friends. It is
barely possible, that such a report might be put in
circulation through error or mistake, and afterwards
gain credit by time; but in my judgment in no degree
probable, when all the circumstances of the case are
duly considered. The family of Doctor Johnes, sons
and daughters, were of mature age, and some of them
active members of society, when this note is said to
have been written, and the fact to which it related
took place. It is scarcely possible that they should
have been deceived; and their characters are too well
known to suppose them willing to deceive others.

Very respectfully yours,
JAMES RICHARDS.[115]

(7) THE LORD'S SUPPER

"It is the Sabbath. The congregation are assembled in an orchard, in a natural basin which
Providence had made for them, to pay their

homage to the Most High, and to commemorate the love of the Redeemer, even in the winter. Among their number is the commander-in-chief of the American army. With a willing and devout spirit he unites with the people of God in the ordinances of religion. After a solemn sermon from a venerable minister, a hymn is sung, and the invitation given to the members of sister churches to unite in the celebration of the Lord's Supper. A well-known military form rises in response to the invitation. With solemn dignity and Christian meekness he takes his seat with Christ's people and partakes of the bread and wine. It is Washington at the communion table."[116]

(8) TESTIMONY OF REV. O. L. KIRTLAND

The following letter of the Rev. O. L. Kirtland, who came to Morristown in 1837, pastor of the Second Presbyterian Church at Morristown, who married into the family of the Rev. Dr. Johnes, was written to the editor of the Presbyterian Magazine in 1851.

REV. AND DEAR BROTHER:

The father of Mrs. Kirtland was the son of the Reverend Doctor Timothy Johnes—lived with him, and took care of him in his old age, and till his death —remained in the homestead of his father, and died there in his 83rd year, November, 1836. Mrs. Kirtland was born in the same house, and never had her home elsewhere till a short time since. She recollects very distinctly that she was accustomed to hear her father speak of the fact that the religious services of the congregation *were conducted in the orchard, in the rear of the house*, whilst Washington was here during the Revolutionary War. This was one of the familiar facts often repeated during her early years. She has no doubt that a part of the familiar subject of the conversation of her father with the family, and with visitors, was, that the communion which General Washington attended was held in the orchard.

In the orchard there is a natural basin several feet deep, and a few rods in diameter. The basin was formerly considerably deeper than at present, having been partly filled in the process of tilling ever since the Revolution. Mrs. Kirtland recollects that her father used to say, that when the people assembled for worship, they occupied the bottom of that basin for their place of meeting. The minister stood on one side of the basin, so as to be elevated above his congregation. The whole field inclines towards the morning and mid-day sun. The rising grounds in the rear would, to a great extent, shield the congregation from the usual winds of winter. Indeed, the basin was formerly so deep, that the wind from any direction would mainly pass over them.

A brother of Mrs. Kirtland, several years older than herself, and other members of the family, tell me that their recollections are distinct, and in harmony with hers, touching the meetings in the orchard, the communion, and the presence of Washington there.

John B. Johnes, M.D., now living in this place [1851], and over sixty years of age, grandson of the old minister, and cousin of Mrs. Kirtland, recollects it as the familiar talk of his father, and also of his uncle, Mrs. Kirtland's father, that the religious services, whilst Washington was here, were in that orchard.[117]

(9) TESTIMONY OF CHARLOTTE MORRELL BRACKETT

Here is an extract from a letter written May 19, 1902, by Charlotte Morrell Brackett, a great-great-granddaughter of Doctor Johnes:

"It is not a matter of tradition only, but of pure authentic history—in fact, a part of the history of the First Presbyterian Church of Morristown—as it was the first pastor of the church, the Reverend Doctor Timothy Johnes (my great-great-grandfather), who administered the rite to Washington. . . . To me it has always been a matter of family history."[118]

(10) WHY SERVICE IN OPEN AIR

"There was a vast amount of sickness and suffering in the army; the smallpox prevailed fearfully, the Presbyterian and Baptist churches, and courthouse, were occupied as hospitals—

the father of Mrs. Kirtland having, the latter part of the time, the supervision of the hospitals —so that there was no place for the meeting of the congregation, except in the open air."[119]

In commemoration of this event the spot has been marked by a sundial, placed there by the Daughters of the American Revolution.

Remained Standing During Service

The Rev. O. L. Kirtland, in his letter to the editor of the Presbyterian Magazine, also mentions the following interesting incident: "Mrs. Scofield, wife of one of our lawyers, and granddaughter of a Mrs. Ford,[120] whose name has been handed down to us fragrant with piety, informs me that her grandmother used to tell her about attending the meetings in the orchard. On one occasion, when the old lady was present, Washington was there sitting in his camp chair, brought in for the occasion. During the service, a woman came into the congregation with a child in her arms; Washington arose from his chair and gave it to the woman with the child."[121] A writer in 1833 says that all the seats were occupied, and Washington remained standing throughout the whole service.

Withdraws from Communion Service

The circumstance of his withdrawing him-

self from the communion service at a certain
period of his life has been remarked as singular.
This may be admitted, and regretted, both on
account of his example, and the value of his
opinion as to the importance and practical ten-
dency of this rite.   It does not follow, however,
that he was an unbeliever, unless the same
charge is proved to rest against the numerous
class of persons, who believe themselves to be
sincere Christians, but who have scruples in
regard to the ordinance of the communion.
Whatever his motives may have been, it does
not appear that they were ever explained.   Nor
is it known, or to be presumed, that any occasion
offered.   It is probable that, after he took command of the army, finding his thoughts and
attention necessarily engrossed by the business
that devolved upon him, in which frequently
little distinction could be observed between the
Sabbath and other days, he may have believed
it improper publicly to partake of an ordinance
which, according to the ideas he entertained of
it, imposed severe restrictions on outward conduct, and a sacred pledge to perform duties
impracticable in his situation. Such an impression would be natural to a serious mind;
and, although it might be an erroneous view
of the nature of the ordinance, it would not
have the less weight with a man of a deli-

cate conscience and habitual reverence. for religion.[122]

Because he was so regular and devoted in his Christian life and habits of devotion, "it was the more noticeable that he ceased to be a regular communicant as long as the war lasted. Washington always had his reasons for what he did, or left undone; but he seldom gave them; and his motive for abstaining from the sacrament was not a subject on which he would be inclined to break his ordinary rule of reticence."[123] His partaking of the communion at Morristown throws some light upon his inward convictions.

VICE AND IMMORALITY DISCOURAGED

In a circular to the brigadier-generals, dated May 26, 1777, are the following instructions:

Let vice and immorality of every kind be discouraged as much as possible in your brigade; and, as a chaplain is allowed to each regiment, see that the men regularly attend divine worship. Gaming of every kind is expressly forbidden, as being the foundation of evil, and the cause of many a brave and gallant officer's ruin. Games of exercise for amusement may not only be permitted but encouraged.[124]

MARK OF PROVIDENCE

In writing to General Armstrong, from Morristown, New Jersey, July 4, 1777, he says:

The evacuation of Jersey [by the British troops] at this time is a peculiar mark of Providence, as the inhabitants have an opportunity of securing their harvests of hay and grain, the latter of which would, in all probability, have undergone the same fate with many farmhouses, had it been ripe enough to take fire. The distress of many of the inhabitants, who were plundered not only of their effects but of their provision of every kind, was such, that I sent down several wagon-loads of meat and flour to supply their present wants.[125]

The reader will observe in this extract striking proof of the writer's unqualified faith in the immediate and particular agency of the Almighty in the affairs of men. By this agency, a plundering army had been forced to leave the agricultural districts of the country at a period the most critical to the farmer. It was near the season of harvest when they evacuated the State, but the grain was in too green a state to be burnt. But for this the dependence for bread in that region would have been cut off. This interposition was indeed "a peculiar mark of Providence," and the reverential notice of it a commendable instance of devout feeling.[126]

DIVINE SERVICE NOT TO BE OMITTED

October 7, 1777, Washington issued the following order:

The situation of the army frequently not admitting
of the regular performance of divine service on Sundays, the chaplains of the army are forthwith to meet
together and agree on some method of performing it
at other times, which method they will make known
to the Commander-in-chief.[127]

SIGNAL STROKE OF PROVIDENCE

To his brother John A. Washington, he writes,
October 18, 1777, announcing the capitulation of
Burgoyne's army at Saratoga, in which he says,
"I most devoutly congratulate my country, and
every well-wisher to the cause, on this signal
stroke of Providence."[128]

SYMPATHY FOR GENERAL PUTNAM

He sent a letter to Major-General Putnam
Sunday, October 19, 1777, in which he says:

The defeat of General Burgoyne is a most important
event, and such as must afford the highest satisfaction to every well-affected American. Should Providence be pleased to crown our arms in the course of
the campaign with one more fortunate stroke, I
think we shall have no great cause for anxiety respecting the future designs of Britain. I trust all
will be well in His good time. . .

The letter closes with a word of sympathy:

I am exceedingly sorry for the death of Mrs. Put-
man, and sympathize with you upon the occasion.
Remembering that all must die, and that she had
lived to an honorable age, I hope you will bear the

misfortune with that fortitude and complacency of mind that become a man and a Christian.[129]

SUPERINTENDING PROVIDENCE

In a letter to Landon Carter, of Sabine Hall, Richmond county, Virginia, October 27, 1777, he says:

I have this instant received an account of the prisoners taken by the northern army (including tories in arms against us) in the course of the campaign. This singular instance of Providence, and of our good fortune under it, exhibits a striking proof of the advantages which result from unanimity and a spirited conduct in the militia. . . . I flatter myself that a superintending Providence is ordering everything for the best, and that, in due time, all will end well.[130]

THANKSGIVING AND PRAISE

He issued the following order on December 17, 1777, near Valley Forge:

To-morrow being the day set apart by the honorable Congress for public thanksgiving and praise, and duty calling us devoutly to express our grateful acknowledgments to God for the manifold blessings he has granted us, the General directs that the army remain in its present quarters, and that chaplains perform divine service with their several corps and brigades; and earnestly exhorts all officers and soldiers, whose absence is not indispensably necessary, to attend with reverence the solemnities of the day.[131]

CHAPTER VII
PRAYER AT VALLEY FORGE

(1) REVEREND MASON L. WEEMS' ACCOUNT

IN the winter of 1777–78, while Washington, with the American army, was encamped at Valley Forge, amidst all the perplexities and troubles and sufferings, the Commander-in-chief sought for direction and comfort from God. He was frequently observed to visit a secluded grove. One day a Tory Quaker by the name of Isaac Potts "had occasion to pass through the woods near headquarters. Treading in his way along the venerable grove, suddenly he heard the sound of a human voice, which, as he advanced, increased in his ear; and at length became like the voice of one speaking much in earnest. As he approached the spot with a cautious step, whom should he behold, in a dark natural bower of ancient oaks, but the Commander-in-chief of the American armies on his knees at prayer! Motionless with surprise, Friend Potts continued on the place till the general, having ended his devotions, arose, and, with a countenance of angelic serenity, retired to headquarters.

Friend Potts then went home, and on entering his parlor called out to his wife, "Sarah! my dear Sarah! All's well! all's well! George Washington will yet prevail."

"What's the matter, Isaac?" replied she; "thee seems moved."

"Well, if I seem moved, 'tis no more than what I really am. I have this day seen what I never expected. Thee knows that I always thought that the sword and the gospel were utterly inconsistent; and that no man could be a soldier and a Christian at the same time. But George Washington has this day convinced me of my mistake."

He then related what he had seen, and concluded with this prophetical remark! "If George Washington be not a man of God, I am greatly deceived—and still more shall I be deceived, if God do not, through him, work out a great salvation for America."[132]

(2) BENSON J. LOSSING'S ACCOUNT

Isaac Potts, at whose house Washington was quartered, relates that one day, while the Americans were encamped at Valley Forge, he strolled up the creek, when, not far from his den, he heard a solemn voice. He walked quietly in the direction of it, and saw Washington's horse tied to a sapling. In a thicket near by was the beloved chief upon his knees in prayer, his cheeks suffused with tears. Like Moses at the bush, Isaac felt the he was upon holy ground, and withdrew unobserved. He was much agitated, and, on entering the room where his wife was, he burst into tears. On her inquiring the cause, he informed her of what he had seen, and added, "If there is anyone on this earth whom the Lord will listen to, it is George Washington; and I feel a presentiment that under such a commander there can be no doubt of our eventually establishing our independence, and that God in his providence has willed it so."[133]

(3) TESTIMONY OF DEVAULT BEAVER

Extract of a letter from a Baptist minister to the editor of the (Boston) Christian Watchman, dated Baltimore, January 13, 1832:

"The meetinghouse (which is built of stone) belonging to the church just alluded to is in sight of the spot on which the American army, under the command of General Washington, was encamped during a most severe winter. This, you know, was then called '*Valley Forge.*' It is affecting to hear the old people narrate the sufferings of the army, when the soldiers were frequently tracked by the blood from the sore and bare feet, lacerated by the rough and frozen roads over which they were obliged to pass.

"You will recollect that a most interesting incident, in relation to the life of the great American commander-in-chief, has been related as follows: That while stationed here with the army he was frequently observed to visit a secluded grove. This excited the curiosity of a Mr. Potts, of the denomination of '*Friends*,' who watched his movements at one of these seasons of retirement, till he perceived that he was on his *knees* and engaged in *prayer*. Mr. Potts then returned, and said to his family, '*Our* cause is *lost*' (he was with the Tories), assigning his reasons for this opinion. There is a man by the name of Devault Beaver, now living on this spot (and is eighty years of age), who says he has this statement from Mr. Potts and his family.

"I had before heard this interesting anecdote in the life of our venerated Washington, but had some misgivings about it, all of which are now fully removed."[134]

(4) TESTIMONY OF DOCTOR SNOWDEN

The following note was written to the Rev. T. W. J. Wylie, D.D., pastor of the First Reformed Presbyterian Church, of Philadelphia, February 28, 1862:

My DEAR SIR—Referring to your request, I have to say that I cannot lay my hands at present upon my father's papers. I recollect that among his manuscript "Reminiscences," was a statement of his interview with Mr. Potts, a Friend, near Valley Forge, who pointed out to him the spot where he saw General Washington at prayer in the winter of 1777. This event induced Friend Potts to become a Whig; and he told his wife Betty, that the cause of America was a good cause, and would prevail, and that they must now support it. Mr. Weems, in his "Life of Washington," mentions this incident a little differently; but my father had it from Mr. Potts personally, and the statement herein made may therefore be relied on as accurate.

I am, with great regard,

Yours truly,

JAMES ROSS SNOWDEN.

Dr. Wylie says, "We have heard the incident just related from the lips of the late Dr. N. R. Snowden, who was informed of it by the person himself."[135]

(5) GENERAL KNOX A WITNESS

It may be added that besides the individual named above as having witnessed the private devotions of General Washington at Valley Forge, it is known that General Knox also was an accidental witness of the same, and was fully apprised that *prayer* was the object of the Commander's frequent visits to the grove. This officer was especially devoted to the person of the Commander-in-chief, and had very free and

familiar access to him, which may in some measure account for his particular knowledge of his
habits.

That an adjacent wood should have been
selected as his private oratory, while regularly
encamped for the winter, may excite the inquiry
of some. The cause may possibly be found in
the fact that, in common with the officers and
soldiers of the army, he lodged during that winter in a log hut, which, from the presence of Mrs.
Washington, and perhaps other inmates, and the
fewness of the apartments, did not admit of that
privacy proper for such a duty.[136]

(6) INDEPENDENCE BORN OF PRAYER

"Few scenes have had so much moral grandeur
in them as this. Repeated disaster and defeat
had disappointed the army and the nation.
Suffering, to an extreme degree, was in the
camp, and thousands of brave men were without
the necessities of life. The independence of the
nation was in jeopardy. Attempts were made
to stab the reputation of the commander, and to
degrade him from office. Provision for the army
was to be made, murmurs and discontents suppressed, calumny to be met, plans formed for a
future campaign, the nation to be inspirited and
aroused; an active enemy was in the neighborhood, flushed with recent victory, and preparing

to achieve new triumphs; and in these circumstances the Father of his Country went alone and sought strength and guidance from the God of armies and light. The ear of Heaven was propitious to his prayer; and who can tell how much of the subsequent brilliant success of the American armies was in answer to the prayers of the American general at Valley Forge? To latest times it will and should be a subject of the deepest interest that the independence of our country was laid, not only in valor and patriotism and wisdom, but in prayer. The example of Washington will rebuke the warrior or the statesman who never supplicates the blessing of God on his country. It will be encouragement for him who prays for its welfare and its deliverance from danger."[137]

"EXAMPLE OF CHRISTIAN CHARITY"

Whileen camped at Valley Forge one day a Tory who was well known in the neighborhood was captured and brought into camp. His name was Michael Wittman, and he was accused of having carried aid and information to the British in Philadelphia. He was taken to West Chester and there tried by court-martial. It was proved that he was a very dangerous man and that he had more than once attempted to do great harm to the American army. He was pronounced guilty of being a spy and sentenced to be hanged.

On the evening of the day before that set for the execution, a strange old man appeared at Valley Forge. He was a small man with long, snow-white hair falling over his shoulders. His face, although full of kindliness, was sad-looking and thoughtful; his eyes, which were bright and sharp, were upon the ground and lifted only when he was speaking. . . .

His name was announced.

"Peter Miller?" said Washington. "Certainly. Show him in at once."

"General Washington, I have come to ask a great favor of you," he said, in his usual kindly tones.

"I shall be glad to grant you almost anything," said Washington, "for we surely are indebted to you for many favors. Tell me what it is."

"I hear," said Peter, "that Michael Wittman has been found guilty of treason and that he is to be hanged at Turk's Head to-morrow. I have come to ask you to pardon him."

Washington started back, and a cloud came over his face.

"That is impossible," he said. "Wittman is a bad man. He has done all in his power to betray us. He has even offered to join the British and aid in destroying us. In these times we dare not be lenient with traitors; and for that reason I cannot pardon your friend."

"Friend!" cried Peter. "Why, he is no friend of mine. He is my bitterest enemy. He has persecuted me for years. He has even beaten me and spit in my face, knowing full well that I would not strike back. Michael Wittman is no friend of mine."

Washington was puzzled. "And still you wish me to pardon him?" he asked.

"I do," answered Peter. "I ask it of you as a great personal favor."

"Tell me," said Washington, with hesitating voice, "why is it that you thus ask the pardon of your worst enemy?"

"I ask it because Jesus did as much for me," was the old man's brief answer.

Washington turned away and went into another room. Soon he returned with a paper on which was written the pardon of Michael Wittman.

"My dear friend," he said, as he placed it in the old man's hands, "I thank you for this example of Christian charity."[138]

ACKNOWLEDGES RECEIPT OF SERMON

On March 13, 1778, he writes from Valley

Forge to the Reverend Israel Evans, acknowledging the receipt of his sermon, as follows:

Your favor of the 17th ultimo, enclosing the Discourse which you delivered on the 18th of December, the day set apart for a general thanksgiving, never came to my hands till yesterday. I have read this performance with equal attention and pleasure; and at the same time that I admire and feel the force of your reasoning which you have displayed through the whole, it is more especially incumbent upon me to thank you for the honorable but partial mention you have made of my character, and to assure you that it will ever be the first wish of my heart to aid your pious endeavors to inculcate a due sense of the dependence we ought to place in the all-wise and powerful Being, on whom alone our success depends.[139]

FASTING

An order issued at Headquarters, Valley Forge, April 12, 1778, includes the following directions for a day of fasting and prayer:

The Honorable the Congress having thought proper to recommend to the United States of America to set apart Wednesday, the 22nd inst., to be observed as a day of Fasting, Humiliation and Prayer, that at one time, and with one voice, the righteous dispensations of Providence may be acknowledged, and His goodness and mercy towards our arms supplicated and implored:

The General directs that the day shall be most religiously observed in the Army; that no work shall be done thereon, and that the several chaplains do prepare discourses suitable to the occasion.[140]

CHRISTIAN ABOVE PATRIOT

The following order was issued at Headquarters, Valley Forge, May 2, 1778:

The Commander-in-chief directs that Divine service be performed every Sunday at 11 o'clock, in each Brigade which has a Chaplain. Those Brigades which have none will attend the places of worship nearest to them.—It is expected that officers of all ranks will, by their attendance, set an example for their men. While we are duly performing the duty of good soldiers we certainly ought not to be inattentive to the higher duties of religion. To the distinguished character of a Patriot it should be our highest glory to add the more distinguished character of a Christian.

The signal instances of Providential goodness which we have experienced, and which have almost crowned our arms with complete success, demand from us, in a peculiar manner, the warmest returns of gratitude and piety to the Supreme Author of all Good.[141]

THANKSGIVING ORDERED

An order issued at Valley Forge, May 5, 1778, begins as follows:

PRAYER AT VALLEY FORGE

It having pleased the Almighty Ruler of the Universe propitiously to defend the cause of the United American States, and finally by raising us up a powerful friend among the Princes of the earth, to establish our Liberty and Independence upon a lasting foundation; it becomes us to set apart a day for gratefully acknowledging the Divine Goodness, and celebrating the event, which we owe to His benign interposition. The several brigades are to be assembled at nine o'clock to-morrow morning, when their Chaplains will communicate the intelligence contained in the Postscript of the Gazette of 2nd inst., and offer up a thanksgiving, and deliver a discourse suitable to the occasion.[142]

"Washington, with his lady, and suite, Lord Stirling and his lady, with other general officers and ladies, attended the religious services of the Jersey brigade, when the Rev. Mr. Hunter delivered a discourse."[143]

RECOGNIZES PROTECTION OF PROVIDENCE

In a letter to Landon Carter, written from Valley Forge, May 30, 1778, he says:

My friends, therefore, may believe me sincere in my professions of attachment to them, whilst Providence has a just claim to my humble and grateful thanks for its protection and direction of me through the many difficult and intricate scenes which this contest has produced; and for its constant interposition in our behalf, when the clouds were heaviest and seemed ready to burst upon us.

To paint the distresses and perilous situation of this army in the course of last winter, for want of clothes, provisions, and almost every other necessary essential to the well-being, I may say existence, of an army, would require more time and an abler pen than mine; nor, since our prospects have so miraculously brightened, shall I attempt it, or even bear it in remembrance, further than as a memento of what is due to the great Author of all the care and good that have been extended in relieving us in difficulties and distresses.[144]

CHAPTER VIII

WASHINGTON NOT PROFANE

(1) BATTLE OF MONMOUTH

AN effort has been made by some, holding infidel views, to bring down Washington to the common level of other men, by conveying the impression that he was in the habit of swearing. He was a man of strong passions, we will allow (and few very great men have been otherwise), but they were wonderfully regulated and controlled by religious principle. Two occasions have been named, when, it is asserted by some, Washington used profane language. One was at the battle of Monmouth and the other was when he received the news of St. Clair's defeat by the Indians. Concerning the incident at Monmouth, the following testimony seems conclusive:

(2) PERSONAL WITNESSES

The following interesting communication from General Joseph G. Swift, of Geneva, New York, will be read with interest:

"I had long ago heard of Washington's using harsh language to Lee at Monmouth (June 28,

1778); and having, in 1804, a letter of introduction to General Marshall, at Richmond, I inquired as to the facts. The general said that the story of coarse language between Washington and Lee *was not true.* General Marshall was captain on the field of Monmouth, and near Washington. He stated that Lee's *language was decorous,* and that Washington's manner and language was austere, but not profane. In the year 1803, I was in Albany with my then chief, Colonel Williams, and there heard General Alexander Hamilton say to General Schuyler and Colonel Williams that the story of General Washington's profanity at Fort Lee, on a visit of inspection, *was not true.* Washington was disappointed at not finding the commandant at his post, and expressed his displeasure in strong language but not with an oath. While a member of General Thomas Pinckney's military family in South Carolina, 1812, I heard his brother, General C. C. Pinckney, frequently mention conversations with General Washington. He said that he was habitually grave in discourse, cautious in expression, slow and accurate in judgment, but with intimate friends, easy, though rarely jocose. Now, General C. C. Pinckney was remarkable for facetiousness and humor, and at the table of his brother was fond of conversing with young men; neither of these

brothers believed the story of Washington's
swearing at Lee. At the meeting of Washington
and Lee, the language of the former might be
more to undo the evil then in progress, than to
expend words on Lee. It is fair to conclude
that Washington's mind, so well known for
coolness in battle, would be far more engaged
in restoring the order of the day in pursuit of
the enemy, than in applying epithets to Lee."[145]

(3) Testimony at the Court-Martial

The scenes and events of that day were the
subject of a prolonged and very critical investigation while the actors in them were still within
reach and, as it were, fresh from the field.
General Lee's trial by a general court-martial,
beginning on the 4th of July, six days after the
battle, ended on the 12th of August, with his
suspension from any command in the armies of
the United States of North America, for the
term of twelve months. The statements of
General Washington and General Lee in the correspondence which led to the court-martial, the
sworn testimony of the witnesses upon the trial,
and the defense of General Lee himself, furnish
conclusive evidence of the utter falsehood of
these pretended traditions which have gained
entrance where they ought never to have been
received for a moment.[146]

(4) STATEMENT OF GENERAL SCOTT

General Charles Scott had a most inveterate habit of swearing; whether in private or public society, on his farm, or the field of battle, every other word was an oath. On the night preceding the battle of Princeton, Scott received an order from the Commander-in-chief in person to defend a bridge to the last extremity. "To the last man, your excellency," replied Scott; and, forgetting the presence of the chief, accompanied the words with tremendous oaths. The general, as may be well supposed, had but little time, on that eventful evening, to notice or chide this want of decorum in his brave and well-tried soldier. After the war, a friend of the gallant general, anxious to reform his evil habits, asked him whether it was possible that the man so much beloved, the admired Washington, ever swore? Scott reflected for a moment, and then exclaimed, "Yes, once. It was at Monmouth, and on a day that would have made any man swear. Yes, sir, he swore on that day, till the leaves shook on the trees, charming, delightful. Never have I enjoyed such swearing before, or since. Sir, on that ever memorable day he swore like an angel from heaven."[147]

It is more than likely that the profane general fully recognized the vast difference between his own language and that of the high-minded

Washington. Hence, he likens him to an "angel," saying, "He swore like an angel from heaven." As much as to say, the provocation was "enough to make an angel swear, but Washington swore no more than an angel from heaven." How would an angel from heaven swear? General Scott really paid the great Washington the highest compliment and in a very delicate manner denied the accusation of profanity.

NEVER-FAILING PROVIDENCE

In a letter to John Augustine Washington, July 4, 1778, telling of the battle of Monmouth and General Lee's retreat, he says:

The disorder arising from it [the retreat] would have proved fatal to the army had not that bountiful Providence, which has never failed us in the hour of distress, enabled me to form a regiment or two [of those that were retreating] in the face of the enemy and under their fires.[148]

WORSE THAN AN INFIDEL

In a letter to Brigadier-General Nelson, of Virginia, written from White Plains, New York, August 20, 1778, he says:

The hand of Providence has been conspicuous in all this, that he must be worse than an infidel that lacks faith, and more than wicked that has not gratitude enough to acknowledge his obligations. But it will be time enough for me to turn preacher when my present appointment ceases; and therefore I shall add no more on the doctrine of Providence.[149]

Morals Irreproachable

In a letter from "a gentleman of Maryland" to a friend in Europe, written May 3, 1779, is the following:

"He is strictly just, vigilant, and generous; an affectionate husband, a faithful friend, a father to the deserving soldiers; gentle in manners, in temper rather reserved; a total stranger to religious prejudices, which have so often excited Christians of one denomination to cut the throats of those of another; in his morals irreproachable; he was never known to exceed the bounds of the most rigid temperance."[150]

Character Sketch

In a sketch written in 1779, "by an American Gentleman now in London, who is well acquainted with him," we find the following:

"He punishes neglect of duty with great severity, but is very tender and indulgent to recruits until they learn the articles of war and their exercises perfectly."

"He regularly attends divine service in his

tent every morning and evening, and seems very fervent in his prayers."

"He is so tender-hearted that no soldiers must be flogged nigh his tent; or if he is walking in the camp and sees a man tied to the halberds, he will either order him to be taken down or walk another way to avoid the sight."

"He is humane to the prisoners who fall into his hands, and orders everything necessary for their relief."[151]

CHAPTER IX

GENERAL WASHINGTON A MAN OF PRAYER

(1) At a Farmer's House

The Rev. E. C. M'Guire, often quoted in this volume, relates an additional example of Washington engaged in prayer as occurring during the war, which, he says, was taken from a respectable literary journal published in New York. It is here inserted as having in its prominent points all the appearance of truth:

"One pleasant evening in the month of June, in the year 1779 (?), a man was observed entering the borders of a wood, near the Hudson River, his appearance that of a person above the common rank. The inhabitants of a country village would have dignified him with the title of squire, and from his manner, have pronounced him proud; but those more accustomed to society would inform you, there was something like a military air about him. His horse panted as if it had been hard pushed for some miles, yet from the owner's frequent stops to caress the patient animal, he could not be charged with want of humanity, but seemed to be actuated by some urgent necessity. The rider's forsaking a good road for the bypath leading through the woods indicated a desire to avoid the gaze of other travelers. He had not left the house where he inquired the direction of the above mentioned path more than two hours before the quietude of the place was broken by the noise of distant thunder. He was soon after obliged to dismount, traveling becoming dangerous, as darkness concealed surrounding objects, except when the lightning's terrific flash afforded a momentary view of his situation. A peal louder and of longer duration than any of the preceding, which now burst over his head, seeming as if it would rend the woods asunder, was quickly followed by a heavy fall of rain, which penetrated the clothing of the stranger ere he could obtain the shelter of a large oak, which stood at a little distance.

"Almost exhausted with the labors of the day, he was about making such disposition of the saddle and his own coat, as would enable him to pass the night with what comfort circumstances would admit, when he espied a light glimmering through the trees. Animated with the hope of better lodgings, he determined to proceed. The way, which was somewhat steep, became attended with more obstacles the farther he advanced, the soil being composed of clay, which the rain had rendered so soft that his feet slipped at every step. By the utmost perseverance, this difficulty was finally overcome without any accident, and he had the pleasure of finding himself in front of a decent looking farmhouse. The watchdog began barking, which brought the owner of the mansion to the door.

" 'Who is there?' said he.

" 'A friend who has lost his way, and in search of a place of shelter,' was the answer.

" 'Come in, sir,' added the first speaker, 'and whatever my house will afford, you shall have with welcome.'

" 'I must first provide for the weary companion of my journey,' remarked the other.

"But the former undertook the task, and after conducting the newcomer into a room where his wife was seated, he led the horse to a well-stored barn, and there provided for him most bountifully. On rejoining the traveler, he observed, 'that is a noble animal of yours, sir.'

" 'Yes,' was the reply, 'and I am sorry that I was obliged to misuse him so, as to make it necessary to give you much trouble with the care of him; but I have yet to thank you for your kindness to both of us.'

" 'I did no more than my duty, sir,' said the entertainer, 'and therefore I am entitled to no thanks. But Susan,' added he, turning to the hostess, with a half-reproachful look, 'why have you not given the gentleman something to eat?'

"Fear had prevented the good woman from exercising her well-known benevolence, for a robbery had been committed by a lawless band of depredators but a few days before, in that neighborhood, and as report stated that the ruffians were all well dressed, her imagination suggested that this man might be one of them.

"At her husband's remonstrance, she now readily engaged in repairing her error, by preparing a plentiful repast. During the meal, there was much interesting conversation among the three. As soon as the worthy countryman perceived that his guest had satisfied his appetite he informed him that it was now the hour at which the family usually performed their evening devotions, inviting him at the same time to be present. The invitation was accepted in these words:

" 'It would afford me the greatest pleasure to commune with my heavenly Preserver, after the events of the day; such exercises prepare us for the repose we seek in sleep.'

"The host now reached his Bible from the shelf, and after reading a chapter and singing, concluded the whole with a fervent prayer; then lighting a pine-knot, conducted the person he had entertained to his chamber, wished him a good night's rest, and retired to the adjoining apartment.

" 'John,' whispered the woman, 'that is a good gentleman, and not one of the highwaymen as I supposed.'

" 'Yes, Susan,' said he, 'I like him better for thinking of his God, than for all his kind inquiries after our welfare. I wish our Peter had been home from the army, if it was only to hear this good man talk; I am sure Washington himself could not say more for his country, nor give a better history of the hardships endured by our brave soldiers.'

" 'Who knows now,' inquired the wife, 'but it may be he himself, after all, my dear, for they do say, he travels just so, all alone, sometimes. Hark! what's that?'

"The sound of a voice came from the chamber of their guest, who was now engaged in his *private religious worship*. After thanking the Creator for his many mercies, and asking a blessing on the inhabitants of the house, he continued: 'And now, Almighty Father, if it is Thy holy will, that we shall obtain a place and a name among the nations of the earth, grant that we may be enabled to show our gratitude for Thy goodness, by our endeavors to fear and obey Thee. Bless us with wisdom in our councils, success in battle, and let all our victories be tempered with

humanity. Endow also our enemies with enlightened minds, that they may become sensible
of their injustice, and willing to restore our liberty and peace.   Grant the petition of Thy servant for the sake of Him whom Thou hast
called Thy Beloved Son; nevertheless, not my
will, but Thine be done.   Amen.'

"The next morning, the traveler, declining
the pressing solicitations to breakfast with his
host, declared it was necessary for him to cross
the river immediately; at the same time offering
a part of his purse, as a compensation for the
attention he had received, which was refused.

" 'Well, sir,' concluded he, 'since you will not
permit me to recompense you for your trouble,
it is but just that I should inform you on whom
you have conferred so many obligations, and
also add to them by requesting your assistance
in crossing the river.   I had been out yesterday,
endeavoring to obtain some information respecting our enemy, and being alone, ventured too far
from the camp; on my return I was surprised by
a foraging party, and only escaped by my knowledge of the roads and the fleetness of my horse.
My name is George Washington.'

"Surprise kept the listener silent for a moment; then, after unsuccessfully repeating the invitation to partake of some refreshment, he
hastened to call two negroes, with whose assist-

ance he placed the horse on a small raft of timber, that was lying in the river near the door, and soon conveyed the General to the opposite side, where he left him to pursue his way to the camp, wishing him a safe and prosperous journey. On his return to the house he found that while he was engaged in making preparations for conveying the horse across the river his illustrious visitor had persuaded his wife to accept a token of remembrance, which the family are proud of exhibiting to this day [1835].''[152]

(2)   ANOTHER INSTANCE

Here is another instance of General Washington's habit of prayer, witnessed during the war:

In the year 1820, a clergyman of his state (Virginia), being in company with Major ———, a relative of General Washington, had an accidental conversation with him on the subject of Christianity. The conversation was of a controversial nature in the beginning, and as no good seemed to ensue, but some warmth of feeling, an effort was made to arrest the unprofitable discussion by an inquiry made of the Major, as to the religious opinions of his distinguished kinsman. This was done in part as knowing his veneration for Washington, and for information too, as he had been captain of the General's bodyguard during a greater part of the war, and possessed the best opportunities of learning his views and habits. In answer to the question, he observed, after hesitating for a moment, "General Washington was certainly a pious man, his opinions being in favor of religion, and his habits all of that character and description." Being further interrogated as to his habits, he replied that his uncle, he knew, was in the habit of praying in private; and with the animation of an old soldier, excited by professional recollections rather than sympathy with the subject, he related the circumstances of the following occurrence:

"While encamped at (year and place forgotten by the writer), New Jersey, a soldier arrived one morning, about daybreak, with despatches for the Commander-in-chief, from a distant division of the army. As soon as his business was known he was directed to me as captain of the bodyguard, to whom he came forthwith, and giving me his papers, I repaired at once to the General's quarters. On my way to his room after reaching the house I had to go along a narrow passage of some length. As I approached his door, it being yet nearly dark, I listened for a moment, when I distinguished it as the General's voice, and in another moment found that he was engaged in audible prayer. As in his earnestness he had not heard my footsteps, or if he heard me did not choose to be interrupted, I retired to the front of the dwelling, till such time as I supposed him unengaged; when returning, and no longer hearing his voice, I knocked at the door, which being promptly opened, I delivered the despatches, received an answer, and dismissed the soldier."[153]

(3) HEARD AT PRAYER

A writer says that the Rev. D. D. Field mentioned to her the following:

"Mrs. Watkins, a daughter of Governor Livingston, being at my house in Stockbridge, some twenty years since [this was published in 1857], said that when she was a girl General Washington lived four months at her father's during the Revolution, and that she had been by the side of his room and heard him at prayer. My impression is that she did this repeatedly. She said that his room was in a distant part of the building, and that she had to pass through several rooms to get by the side of the General's room. She stated that her sisters used to go with her and listen, and that their father, learning what they were doing, checked them for it."[154]

(4) SAW HIM ON HIS KNEES

General Robert Porterfield, who was brigade-inspector under General Washington in the

Revolution, told General S. H. Lewis that "upon one occasion, some emergency (which he mentioned) induced him to dispense with the usual formality, and he went directly to General Washington's apartment, where he found him on his knees, engaged in morning devotions. He said that he mentioned the circumstances to General Hamilton, who replied that such was his constant habit."[155]

(5) ANOTHER WITNESS

Mr. Cornelius Doremus, who as a boy was fond of waiting on Washington, who lived part of a winter (1781) at his father's house in Pequannock, New Jersey, states that his bedchamber was directly over that of the Commander-in-chief, and that he often distinctly heard the sound of that deep and earnest voice in private prayer.[156]

(6) DAILY PRAYER

"Throughout the war, as it was understood in his military family, he gave a part of every day to private prayer and devotion."[157]

REGULAR ATTENDANT AT DIVINE SERVICE

The interruptions which sometimes occurred, preventing divine service being performed in camp, did not interfere with attention to the duty on the part of the Commander-in-chief, for one of his secretaries, Judge Harrison, has often been heard to say that "whenever the General could be spared from camp on the Sabbath, he never failed riding out to some neighboring church, to join those who were publicly worshiping the Great Creator."[158]

"During the war he not unfrequently rode ten or twelve miles from camp to attend public worship; and he never omitted this attendance when opportunity presented."[159]

OPEN-AIR SERVICE

In Thacher's Military Journal is found a record of a religious service in the open field on Sunday, July 23, 1780, as follows: "I attended a sermon preached by Mr. Blair, chaplain of the artillery. The troops were paraded in the open field, the sermon was calculated to inculcate religious principles and the moral virtues. His Excellency General Washington, Major-Generals Greene and Knox, with a number of other officers, were present."[160]

CHAPTER X

WASHINGTON AND DIVINE PROVIDENCE

PROVIDENCE HIS ONLY DEPENDENCE

WRITING to William Gordon, March 9, 1781, from Newport, Rhode Island, he says:

We have, as you very justly observe, abundant reasons to thank Providence for its many favorable interpositions in our behalf. It has at times been my only dependence, for all other resources seemed to have failed us.[161]

HAND OF PROVIDENCE RECOGNIZED

Writing to Major-General Armstrong, March 26, 1781, he says:

Our affairs are brought to a perilous crisis, that the hand of Providence, I trust, may be more conspicuous in our deliverance. The many remarkable interpositions of the Divine government in the hours of our deepest distress and darkness, have been too luminous to suffer me to doubt the happy issue of the present contest; but the period for its accomplishment may be too far distant for a person of my years, who in his morning and evening hours, and every moment unccupied by business, pants for retirement, and for those domestic and rural enjoyments, which in my estimation far surpass the highest pageantry of this world.[162]

ATTENDS CHURCH WITH WASHINGTON

Governor Jonathan Trumbull tells in his diary of attending church with Washington on Sunday, May 20th, 1781, at Wethersfield, Connecticut: "Attended divine service with General Washington per tot diem [through the whole day]. Mr. Marshall preached. Matt. 7:3, 'Blessed are the poor in spirit, for theirs is the kingdom of heaven.' "[163]

THANKSGIVING SERVICE AFTER CORNWALLIS' SURRENDER

The closing part of the orders issued by General Washington to the army the day after the capitulation of Yorktown, October 20, 1781, is as follows:

Divine service is to be performed to-morrow in the several brigades or divisions. The Commander-in-chief earnestly recommends that the troops not on duty should universally attend with that seriousness of deportment and gratitude of heart which the recognition of such reiterated and astonishing interposition of Providence demands of us.[164]

ADOPTS CHILDREN

John Parke Custis, his step-son, and the only

son of Mrs. Washington, was aide-de-camp to General Washington at the siege of Yorktown. He was seized with a violent attack of camp-fever, and removed to Eltham, Virginia, thirty miles from Yorktown, to the home of Colonel Bassett, who married Mrs. Washington's sister. After the surrender of Cornwallis, Washington hastened to his bedside. Mrs. Washington was already there. He was present at his death, November 5, 1781. "The chief bowed his head, and in tears gave vent to his deep sorrow; then turning to the weeping mother, he said, 'I adopt the two younger children as my own'" [Eleanor Parke and George Washington Parke Custis, the former usually called "Nelly"].[165]

Belief in Overruling Providence

He writes from Mount Vernon to the President of Congress, November 15, 1781, as follows:

Sir, I have the honor to acknowledge receipt of your favor of the 31st ultimo, covering the resolutions of Congress of the 29th, and a proclamation for a day of public prayer and thanksgiving; and have to thank you, sir, most sincerely, for the very polite and affectionate manner in which those enclosures have been conveyed. The success of the combined arms against our enemies at York and Gloucester, as it affects the welfare and independence of the United States, I viewed as a most fortunate event. In performing my part towards its accomplishment, I consider myself to have done only my duty, and in the execution of that, I ever feel myself happy; and at the same time, as it augurs well to our cause, I take a particular pleasure in acknowledging that the interposing hand of Heaven, in the various instances of our extensive preparations for this operation, has been most conspicuous and remarkable.[166]

INTEMPERANCE DISCOURAGED

While intoxicating liquor was in general use in Washington's time, being regarded as beneficial, he discouraged intemperance in the army, as shown in the following "order," issued at Headquarters, Newburgh, New York, May 16, 1782:

The General is extremely concerned to learn that an article so salutary as that of distilled liquor was expected to be when properly used, and which was designed for the refreshment and comfort of the troops, has been in many instances productive of very ill consequences.

He calls the attention of officers of every grade to remedy these abuses, and to watch over the health of their men; for which purpose he suggests the expedient of keeping liquor rolls in every corps, from which the name of every soldier shall be struck off who addicts himself to drunkenness, or injures his constitution by intemperance.

Such soldiers as are struck off are not to draw liquor on any occasion, but are to receive other articles in lieu thereof. The Quartermasters, upon receiving commuted articles, are to receipt for the full amount of rations included in the returns, that there may be no irregularity in the returns. The evil practice of swallowing the whole ration of liquor at a single draught is also to be prevented, by causing the sergeants to see it duly distributed daily, and mixed with water at stated times; in which case, instead of being pernicious, it will become very refreshing and salutary. An object so essential to the health of the men ought not only to be superintended by the officers of police, but to be deemed worthy to attract the attention of every officer who is anxious for the reputation of the corps to which he belongs, the welfare of individuals, and the good of the service. But it rests principally with the commandants of corps to have so useful a regulation carried effectually into execution, as well as to observe cleanliness and economy and good order within the spheres of their respective commands.

Major-General Heath will be pleased to settle with the brigadiers and commanding officers of brigades, the quantity of liquor proper to be drawn in kind by the troops; after which, he is authorized to commute, by agreement with the contractors, the rations of whiskey, or such proportion of them, as may be judged necessary, for vegetables or other articles, agreeably to the prices fixed in the contract to the component parts of a ration.[167]

Not Waiting for Miracles

In a "Circular to the States," dated Philadel-

phia, January 31, 1782, addressed to Meshech
Weare, President of New Hampshire, occur the
following sentiments:

Although we cannot, by the best concerted plans,
absolutely command success; although the race is
not always to the swift, nor the battle to the strong;
yet, without presumptuously waiting for miracles
to be wrought in our favor, it is our indispensable
duty, with the deepest gratitude to Heaven for the
past, and humble confidence in its smiles on our
future operations, to make use of all the means in our
power for our defense and security.[168]

DIVINE SERVICE EVERY SUNDAY

While encamped at Newburgh, New York, he
gave the following order, Saturday, February
15, 1783:

The New Building being so far finished as to admit
the troops to attend public worship therein, after
to-morrow it is directed that divine service should be
performed there every Sunday by the several chaplains of the New Windsor Cantonment in rotation.[169]

COMMENDS THE CHAPLAINS

March 22, 1783, in the Orderly Book, Newburgh, New York, appears the following:

In justice to the zeal and ability of the Chaplains,
as well as to his own feelings, the Commander-in-
Chief thinks it a duty to declare that the regularity

and decorum with which Divine Service is performed every Sunday, will reflect great credit on the army in general, tend to improve the morals, and the same time increase the happiness of the soldiery, and must afford the most pure, rational entertainments for every serious and well-disposed mind.[170]

REGARD FOR CLERGY

"The high respect in which the clergy of the American army was held by Washington was known to every officer and soldier in the ranks."[171]

THANKSGIVING IN THE ARMY ORDERED

April 18, 1783, on proclaiming to the army the cessation of hostilities, at the end of the war, he said in the general orders:

The proclamation, which will be communicated herewith, will be read tomorrow evening at the head of every regiment and corps in the army; after which the chaplains with the several brigades will render thanks to Almighty God for all his mercies, particularly for his overruling the wrath of man to his own glory, and causing the rage of war to cease among the nations.[172]

VALEDICTORY MESSAGE TO THE GOVERNORS OF THE STATES

From his Headquarters at Newburgh, New York, Sunday, June 8, 1783, General Washington issued a circular letter on disbanding the army, which was addressed to the governors of all the States. The following extracts show his deep religious sentiments:

When we consider the magnitude of the prize we contended for, the doubtful nature of the contest, and the favorable manner in which it has terminated, we shall find the greatest possible reason for gratitude and rejoicing. This is a theme that will afford infinite delight to every benevolent and liberal mind, whether the event in contemplation be considered as the source of present enjoyment or the parent of future happiness; and we shall have equal occasion to felicitate ourselves on the lot which Providence has assigned us, whether we view it in a natural, a political, or moral point of light. . . .

They [the citizens of America] are from this period to be considered as the actors on a most conspicuous theatre, which seems to be peculiarly designated by Providence for the display of human greatness and felicity. Here they are not only surrounded with everything, which can contribute to the completion of private and domestic enjoyment, but Heaven has crowned all its other blessings, by giving a fairer opportunity for political happiness, than any other nation has ever been favored with. . . . The free cultivation of letters, the unbounded extension of commerce, the progressive refinement of manners, the growing liberality of sentiment and, above all, the pure and benign light of Revelation, have had a meliorating influence on mankind and increased the blessings of society.

.   .   .   .

It remains, then, to be my final and only request, that your Excellency will communicate these sentiments to your Legislature at their next meeting, and that they may be considered as the legacy of one who has ardently wished, on all occasions, to be useful to his country, and who, even in the shade of retirement, will not fail to implore the Divine benediction upon it. I now make it my earnest prayer, that God would have you and the State over which you preside, in his Holy protection; that He would incline the hearts of the citizens to cultivate a spirit of subordination and obedience to government; to entertain a brotherly affection and love for one another, for their fellow citizens of the United States at large, and particularly for their brethren who have served in the field; and finally, that He would most graciously be pleased to dispose us all to do justice, to love mercy, and to demean ourselves with that charity, humility, and pacific temper of mind, which are the characteristics of the Divine Author of our blessed religion, and without an humble imitation of whose example in these things we can never hope to be a happy nation.[173]

Thanks God

Washington never failed to render thanks unto God for his guidance. August 26, 1783, he appeared before Congress, in session at Princeton, New Jersey. General Washington entered the hall of Congress, and a brief address was made to him by the President. In his response General Washington said:

Notwithstanding Congress seems to estimate the value of my life beyond any services I have been able to render the United States, yet I must be permitted to consider the wisdom and unanimity of our national councils, the firmness of our citizens, and the patience and bravery of our troops, who have produced so happy a termination of the war, as the most conspicuous effect of the Divine interposition, and the surest presage of our future happiness. . . .

Perhaps, sir, no occasion may offer more suitable than the present to express my humble thanks to God, and my grateful acknowledgments to my country, for the great and uniform support I have received in every vicissitude and fortune, and for the many distinguished honors which Congress has been pleased to confer upon me in the course of the war.[174]

UNDER THE CONTROL OF PROVIDENCE

During the war Washington established headquarters at nearly two hundred and fifty houses, which in eight years averages about twelve days to a house. He longed to retire to his home and private life. Addressing sundry individuals and bodies of men, near the close of the war, he uses the following language:

I anticipate with pleasure the day, and that I trust not far off, when I shall quit the busy scenes of a military employment and retire to the more tran-

1783]   142   [Age 51

quil walks of domestic life. In that, or whatever other situation Providence may dispose my future days, the remembrance of the many friendships and connections I have had the happiness to contract with the gentlemen of the army, will be one of my most grateful reflections. Under this contemplation, and impressed with the sentiments of benevolence and regard, I commend you, my dear sir, my other friends, and with them the interest and happiness of our dear country, to the keeping and protection of Almighty God.[175]

THANKSGIVING FOR TREATY OF PEACE

October 31, 1783, General and Mrs. Washington, and many other distinguished people, attended the services in Princeton College Chapel, in celebration and thanksgiving for the signing at. Versailles, September 3, of the "Definitive Treaty of Peace" between the United States and Great Britain. "The official Proclamation of Peace was the signal for rejoicing that beggars description."[176]

MILITARY FAREWELL ADDRESS

In his farewell address to the armies of the United States at Rock Hill, near Princeton, New Jersey, November, 1783, he does not fail to express again in unmistakable terms his recognition of divine guidance and help:

The singular interpositions of Providence in our

feeble conditions were such as could scarcely escape
the attention of the most observing.

. . . .

And being now to conclude these his last orders, to
take his [Washington's] ultimate leave in a short time
of the military character, and to bid a final adieu to
the armies he has so long had the honor to command,
he can only again offer in their behalf his recommen-
dations to their grateful country, and his prayers to
the God of armies. May ample justice be done
them here, and may the choicest of Heaven's favors,
both here and hereafter, attend those who, under
Divine auspices, have secured innumerable blessings
for others. With these wishes and this benediction,
the Commander-in-chief is about to retire from service. The curtain of separation will soon be drawn,
and the military scene to him will be closed forever.[177]

Thanksgiving for End of War

December 11, 1783, General and Mrs. Washington, at Philadelphia, took part in the service
of thanksgiving which had been recommended
by Congress on the eighteenth of October, to
be observed upon the ending of the great
struggle.[178]

Resigns His Commission

In his address to Congress on resigning his
commission at Annapolis, Maryland, December
23, 1783, his last official act as Commander-in-

chief, once more he acknowledges the guidance and protection of Providence:

Happy in the confirmation of our independence and sovereignty, and pleased with the opportunity offered the United States of becoming a respectable nation, I resign with satisfaction the appointment I accepted with diffidence, a diffidence in my abilities to accomplish so arduous a task, which, however, was superseded by a confidence in the rectitude of our cause, the support of the supreme power of the Union, and the patronage of Heaven.

The successful termination of the war has verified the most sanguine expectations; and my gratitude for the interposition of Providence, and the assistance I have received from my countrymen, increases with every review of the momentous contest.

. . . .

I consider it an indispensable duty to close this last solemn act of my official life, by commending the interests of our dearest country to the protection of Almighty God, and those who have the superintendence of them to His holy keeping.[179]

CHAPTER XI
CHURCH ATTENDANCE AT HOME
CHRISTMAS AT CHURCH

DURING the eight years of the war Washington visited Mount Vernon only twice. The first was on Sunday, the 9th of September, 1781, on his way south for the campaign against Cornwallis. After an absence of six years he remained only three days, leaving on the 12th. The other time was after the surrender of Cornwallis, stopping for a week on his way north again. Immediately after resigning his commission as Commander-in-chief he returns to Mount Vernon, arriving on Christmas Eve, Wednesday, December 24, 1783. The next day he attends church at Alexandria, in the Episcopal church, where he owned a pew, purchased ten years before, "and no one bowed in deeper gratitude than the great general, who came as humbly as a little child to this, his Father's house. In addition to the Christmas service, the rector, the Reverend David Griffith, who served as chaplain of the Third Virginia Regiment in the Revolutionay war, read the exultant song of Moses and the children of Israel: 'I will sing unto the Lord, for he hath triumphed gloriously: the horse and his rider hath he thrown into the sea'; and the sermon he preached was from the 128th Psalm: 'Yea, thou shalt see thy children's children and peace upon Israel.' "[180]

SUPPORTING THE MINISTRY

The following interesting document will furnish very striking proof of his unfeigned desire for the respectable support of the Christian ministry, and perpetual maintenance of religious institutions and services. The design of the paper was, as the reader will observe, to subject the pews of the church to an annual rent, by a voluntary subscription thereto on the part of the pewholders. Its language is:

"We, the subscribers, do hereby agree that the pews we now hold in the Episcopal church at Alexandria, shall be forever charged with an annual rent of five pounds, Virginia money, each; and we hereby promise to pay (each for himself separately promising to pay), annually, forever, to the minister and vestry of the Protestant Episcopal Church in Fairfax parish; or, if the parish should be divided, to the minister and vestry of the Protestant Episcopal Church in Alexandria, the said sum of five pounds for each pew, for the purpose of supporting the ministry in the said church: Provided, nevertheless, that if any law of this Commonwealth should here-after compel us, our heirs, executors, adminis-trators, or assigns, to pay to the support of re-ligion, the pew rent hereby granted, shall, in that case, be considered as part of what we may by such law be required to pay: Provided, also, that each of us pay only in proportion to the part we hold of the said pews. For the performance of which payment, well and truly to be made, for-ever, annually, within six months after demanded, we hereby bind ourselves (each for himself separ-ately), our heirs, executors, administrators, and as-signs, firmly by these presents. In witness where-of, we have hereunto set our hands and seals, this 25th day of April, in the year of our Lord 1785."

The above is an attested copy of the original, now on record in the vestry book of Christ Church, Alexandria. The article was signed by a number of the pewholders, the name of "G. Washington" being at the head of the list, in his own handwriting, with the seal attached.[181]

MEMBER OF CHURCH

His adopted son says, "Washington was a member in full communion of the Protestant Episcopal Church."[182]

FAMILY PRAYERS

"Washington had prayers morning and evening

and was regular in attendance at the church in which he was a communicant."[183]

How He Spent Sunday

"Every Sunday morning the family went to church (when the weather and the roads permitted a ride of ten miles), and in the evening, the general read a sermon, or something else appropriate to the day, for the benefit of the household."[184]

His adopted son says: "Washington was a strict and decorous observer of the Sabbath. He always attended divine service in the morning and read a sermon or some portion of the Bible to Mrs. Washington in the afternoon."[185]

Does Not Forget Falls Church

"Mr. John Lynch, now an old man, who once served the Falls Church as sexton for over forty years, told the writer that in his younger days he learned from a number of aged persons that it was Washington's custom, while giving his regular attendance to Christ Church, Alexandria, also to visit and worship at the Falls Church at least four times a year, this being part of his parish. The particular pew and place in church he usually occupied were said to have been marked and kept for him. . . .

"Several residents of this village now living,

149

whose mother, Mrs. Sarah Maria Sewell, died
many years since at the age of ninety-seven,
still delight and repeat her description of the
great hero, whom in her childhood she had seen
worshiping in this church. She remembered
also his dining occasionally at her home near the
church, and his taking her up in his arms and
playfully caressing her."[186]

DISPENSER OF HUMAN EVENTS

In a letter to Major-General Knox, written
from Mount Vernon, February 20, 1784, he says:

I feel now, however, as I conceive a wearied
traveler must do who, after treading many a painful
step with a heavy burden on his shoulders, is eased
of the latter, having reached the haven to which all
the former were directed; and from his housetop is
looking back, and tracing with an eager eye the
meanders by which he escaped the quicksands and
mires which lay in his way; into which none but
the all-powerful Guide and Dispenser of human
events could have prevented his falling.[187]

ENTERTAINS MINISTERS

In his diary is the following entry:

1785. Sunday, October 2—Went with Fanny
Bassett, Burwell Bassett, Doctor Stuart, G. A.
Washington, Mr. Shaw & Nelly Custis to the Pohick
Church; to hear a Mr. Thompson preach, who

returned home with us to dinner, where I found
Reverend Mr. Jones [David Jones of Chester Co.,
Pa.], formerly a chaplain in one of the Pennsylvania
Regiments.[188]

WANTS SLAVERY ABOLISHED

In a letter to John F. Mercer, September 9,
1786, written from Mount Vernon, he says:

I never mean, unless some particular circumstances should compel it, to possess another slave by
purchase, it being among my first wishes to see some
plan adopted, by which slavery in this country may
be abolished by law.[189]

POHICK CHURCH AGAIN

He writes in his diary, Sunday, October 15,
1786, "Accompanied by Major Washington, his
wife—Mr. Lear and the two children Nelly and
Washington Custis—went to Pohick Church and
returned to dinner."[190]

THE REV. MASON L. WEEMS AT MOUNT VERNON

It has been claimed by some that the Rev.
Mr. Weems, author of the cherry tree and
hatchet story, never met Washington, but in
this they are mistaken. After the Revolution,
Mr. Weems preached at Pohick Church. Washington's diary records that he attended church
there several times during this period, at which
time, no doubt, Mr. Weems was the preacher.

On one occasion at least, Mr. Weems was entertained at Mount Vernon, of which the following
entry in Washington's diary is indisputable evidence: "Saturday, March 3, 1787—The Rev.
Mr. Weems and ye Doctor Craik who came here
yesterday in the afternoon left about noon for
Port Tobacco [Maryland]."[191]

PRESIDENT OF CONSTITUTIONAL CONVENTION

May 25, 1787, Washington was elected "President of the Constitutional Convention," which
met in Philadelphia. When he took the chair,
he said, "Let us raise the standard to which the
wise and honest can repair; the event is in the
hands of God."[192]

GOES TO CHURCH

From the following entries in his diary we
learn that during the convention he did not
neglect attendance at church:

1787. May 26 [Saturday]—Went to the Romish
Church to high mass.[193]

Sunday, June 17, Went to [Christ] Church—
heard Bishop White preach, and see him ordain two
gentlemen Deacons.[194]

PRAYER FOR CONTINUED PROTECTION OF PROVIDENCE

In a letter to Jonathan Trumbull, written
from Mount Vernon, July 20, 1787, he says:

Your friend Colonel Humphreys informs me, from the wonderful revolution of sentiment in favor of federal measures, and the marvelous change for the better in the elections of the State, that he shall begin to suspect that miracles have not ceased. Indeed, for myself, since so much liberality has been displayed in the construction and adoption of the proposed general government, I am almost disposed to be of the same opinion. Or at least we may, with a kind of pious and grateful exultation, trace the fingers of Providence through those dark and mysterious events which first induced the States to appoint a general convention, and then led them one after another, by such steps as were best calculated to effect the object into an adoption of the system recommended by that general convention; thereby in all human probability laying a lasting foundation for tranquillity and happiness, when we had but too much reason to fear that confusion and misery were coming rapidly upon us. That the same good Providence may still continue to protect us, and prevent us from dashing the cup of national felicity, just as it has been lifted to our lips, is the earnest prayer of, my dear sir, your faithful friend, etc., etc.[195]

TOLERATION IN RELIGION

In a letter to the Marquis de Lafayette, written from Philadelphia, August 15, 1787, he says:

I am not less ardent in my wish that you may succeed in your plan of toleration in religious matters.

Being no bigot myself to any mode of worship, I am disposed to indulge the professors of Christianity in the church with that road to Heaven which to them shall seem the most direct, plainest and easiest, and the least liable to exception.[196]

Goes to Pohick Church

Although an attendant at the Episcopal church at Alexandria, we learn from an occasional entry in his diary that he did not lose interest in the old church at Pohick: "Sunday, October 28 [1787]—Went to Pohick church—Mr. Lear and Washington Custis in the carriage with me."[197]

Church at Alexandria

We know from the diaries of some of his contemporaries that Washington did not note in his diary every time he attended church, nor is it clear that there was always a particular reason for mentioning the fact of going to church. However, the entries are very interesting: "Sunday, April 13 [1788]—Went to church at Alexandria, accompanied by Col. Humphrey, Mr. Lear and Washington Custis."[198]

Panic in Church

While visiting his mother at Fredericksburg, Virginia, he attends the village church. The people, knowing he was to be there, crowded into the church until it seemed that the floor would give way. In his diary we find this record for Sunday, June 15, 1788:

On Sunday we went to church—the congregation being alarmed (without cause) and supposing the gallery at the north end was about to fall, were thrown into the utmost confusion; and in the precipitate retreat to the doors many got hurt.[199]

OMNIPOTENT BEING NEVER DESERTED AMERICA

Writing from Mount Vernon to James McHenry, July 31, 1788, he says in closing: "I earnestly pray that the Omnipotent Being, who has not deserted the cause of America in the hour of its extremest hazard, may never yield so fair a heritage of freedom a prey to anarchy or despotism."[200]

AN HONEST MAN

Writing to Alexander Hamilton from Mount Vernon, August 28, 1788, he closes with this: "Still I hope I shall always possess firmness and virtue enough to maintain what I consider the most enviable of all titles, the character of *an honest man*."[201]

RIGHT VS. POPULARITY

In a letter to Henry Lee, in Congress, written

from Mount Vernon, September 22, 1788, in reply to a letter urging him to accept the presidency, he says:

Nor will you conceive me to be solicitous for reputation. Though I prize as I ought the good opinion of my fellow citizens, yet, if I know myself, I would not seek to retain popularity at the expense of one social duty or moral virtue.

While doing what my conscience informed me was right, as it respected my God, my country, and myself, I could despise all the party clamor and unjust censure which might be expected from some whose personal enmity might be occasioned by their hostility to the government.[202]

GOES TO POHICK CHURCH AGAIN

In his diary for Sunday, October 26, 1788, he writes: "Went to Pohick Church and returned home to dinner."[203]

HIS LAST VISIT TO HIS MOTHER

Just before his departure for New York to take the oath of office, and to enter upon his new duties, Washington, actuated by that filial reverence and regard which always distinguished him, hastened to Fredericksburg to visit his mother. She was then four score and two years old, bowed with age and the ravages of that terrible disease, a deep-rooted cancer in the breast. Their interview was deeply affecting.

After the first emotions incident to the meeting had subsided, Washington said: "The people, Madam, have been pleased, with the most flattering unanimity, to elect me to the chief magistracy of these United States; but before I can assume the functions of my office, I have come to bid you an affectionate farewell. So soon as the public business, which must necessarily be encountered in arranging a new government, can be disposed of, I shall hasten to Virginia, and—"

Here the matron interrupted him with, "And you will see me no more. My great age, and the disease which is fast approaching my vitals, warn me that I shall not be long in this world. I trust in God that I may be somewhat prepared for a better. But go, George, fulfill the high destinies which Heaven appears to have intended you for; go, my son, and may that Heaven's and a mother's blessing be with you always."

Washington wept. His head rested upon the shoulder of his mother, whose aged arm feebly, yet fondly encircled his neck. The great man was again a little child, and he kissed the furrowed cheek of his parent with all the tender affection and simplicity of a loving boy. With full heart he went forth to "fulfill the destiny" which heaven assigned him, and he saw his mother no more.[204]

GEORGE WASHINGTON THE CHRISTIAN

Takes No Credit to Himself

In an address to mayor, recorder, aldermen and Common Council of the city of Philadelphia, at a great civic banquet, April 20, 1789, in reply to a congratulatory address on his election to be President, he says:

When I contemplate the interposition of Providence, as it was manifested in guiding us through the Revolution, in preparing us for the reception of a general government, and in conciliating the good will of the people of America towards one another after its adoption, I feel myself oppressed and almost overwhelmed with a sense of the divine munificence. I feel that nothing is due to my personal agency in all these complicated and wonderful events, except what can simply be attributed to the exertions of an honest zeal for the good of my country.

If I have distressing apprehensions, that I shall not be able to justify the too exalted expectations of my countrymen, I am supported under the pressure of such uneasy reflections by a confidence that the most gracious Being, who has hitherto watched over the interests and averted the perils of the United States, will never suffer so fair an inheritance to become a prey to anarchy, despotism, or any other species of oppression.[205]

CHAPTER XII

A CHRISTIAN PRESIDENT

Inauguration

Thursday, April 30, 1789, was the day of inauguration. At nine o'clock in the morning, religious services were held in the churches, and God's blessing invoked in behalf of the new government. At twelve, the President-elect moved in procession to Federal Hall, in Wall Street, where the United States Sub-Treasury Building, formerly the customhouse, now stands, and was received at the door and conducted to the chair by Mr. Adams, the Vice-President. A solemn silence prevailed when Mr. Adams rose and informed him that all things were prepared for him to take the oath of office required by the constitution. Washington then proceeded to a balcony in front of the senate chamber, in view of an immense crowd of people, who hailed him with loud applause. He laid his hand upon his heart, and having bowed several times, he took his seat in an armchair, near a table covered with crimson velvet, on which a superbly bound Bible had been placed.

Washington was dressed in a full suit of dark

brown cloth, with white silk stockings, all of American manufacture, silver shoe-buckles, his hair tied and powdered, and a steel-hilted dress sword by his side.

After a few moments he rose and came forward to the front of the balcony, Mr. Otis, the secretary of state, holding up the Bible on its crimson cushion.

Chancellor Livingston, of New York, administered the oath, which was read slowly and distinctly, Washington laying his hand on the open Bible, and at the conclusion, answering with great solemnity, "I swear—so help me God!" He then bowed down reverently and kissed the Bible.

The chancellor now stepped forward, waved his hand, and said, "Long live George Washington, President of the United States."

The crowds below sent up a loud shout of joy, while the merry peal of church bells and the roar of artillery spread the news abroad, that the birth of a new nation was accomplished.

Returning to the senate chamber, the President delivered his inaugural address, and then proceeded with the whole assembly on foot to Saint Paul's Church, where divine service was celebrated by Mr. Samuel Provoost, Bishop of the Protestant Episcopal Church in New York,

G. Washington

MARTHA WASHINGTON

POHICK CHURCH, VIRGINIA

THE FIRST PRAYER IN CONGRESS

X George Washington.

WASHINGTON RECEIVING COMMUNION
Original Painting in Presbyterian Hospital, Philadelphia, Pa.
(By courtesy of the Superintendent.)

WASHINGTON'S PRAYER AT VALLEY FORGE

CHRIST CHURCH, ALEXANDRIA, VIRGINIA

WASHINGTON AND HIS MOTHER
By courtesy of Mr. Henry F. Scheetz, Philadelphia, Pa.,
owner of original steel engraving.

ST. PAUL'S CHAPEL, NEW YORK

CHRIST CHURCH, PHILADELPHIA

PORTRAIT OF WASHINGTON

Painted from life in 1794.   In Masonic uniform.
Original painting in Masonic Lodge, Alexandria, Va.

Mrs. Washington said after his death that it was the
best picture of him, showing the *real* Washington, not
the idealized Washington.

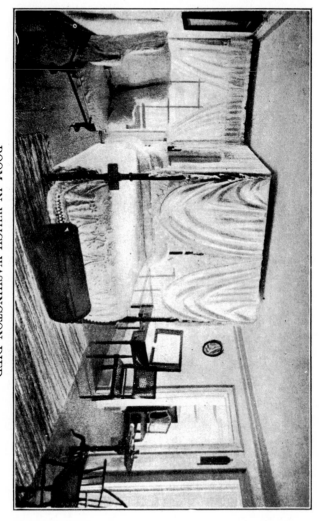

ROOM IN WHICH WASHINGTON DIED

who had been appointed by the Senate one of the chaplains of Congress.[206]

First Inaugural Address

The first inaugural address was delivered to both Houses of Congress, April 30, 1789. It was in part as follows:

Such being the impressions under which I have, in obedience to the public summons, repaired to the present station, it would be peculiarly improper to omit, in this first official act, my fervent supplications to that Almighty Being, who rules over the universe, who presides in the councils of nations, and whose providential aids can supply every human defect, that His benediction may consecrate to the liberties and happiness of the people of the United States a government instituted by themselves for these essential purposes and may enable every instrument employed in its administration to execute with success the functions allotted to his charge. In tendering this homage to the great Author of every public and private good, I assure myself that it expresses your sentiments not less than my own, nor those of my fellow citizens at large, less than either. . . . No people can be bound to acknowledge and adore the invisible hand which conducts the affairs of men more than the people of the United States. Every step by which they have advanced to the character of an independent nation seems to have been distinguished by some token of providential agency. . . . These reflections, arising out of the present crisis, have forced themselves too strongly on my mind to be suppressed. You will join with me, I trust, in thinking that there are none, under the influence of which the proceedings of a new and free government can more auspiciously commence. . . . We ought to be no less persuaded that the propitious smiles of Heaven can never be expected on a nation that disregards the eternal rules of order and right, which Heaven itself has ordained. Having thus imparted to you my sentiments, as they have been awakened by the occasion which brings us together, I shall take my present leave; but not without resorting once more to the benign Parent of the human race, in humble supplication that, since He has been pleased to favor the American people with opportunities for deliberating in perfect tranquillity, and dispositions for deciding with un-paralleled unanimity on a form of government for the security of their union and the advancement of their happiness, so His divine blessing may be equally conspicuous in the enlarged views, the tem-perate consultations, and the wise measures, on which the success of this government may depend.[207]

GRACE AT STATE DINNER

Mrs. Washington left Mount Vernon for New York on the 19th of May, 1789. On her arrival the President gave a semi-official dinner. From one who was present (Mr. Wingate) we have the following account:

A CHRISTIAN PRESIDENT

"The guests consisted of the Vice-President, the foreign ministers, the heads of departments, the speaker of the House of Representatives, and the senators from New Hampshire and Georgia, the then most Northern and Southern States. It was the least showy dinner that I ever saw at the President's table, and the company was not large. As there was no chaplain present, the President himself said a very short grace as he was sitting down."[208]

ADDRESS TO METHODIST EPISCOPAL CHURCH

After his inauguration many formal addresses were sent to President Washington by the various religious societies. His replies form an illuminating commentary on his religious character.

The following address was delivered to the bishops of the Methodist Episcopal Church in the United States in May, 1789:

Gentlemen I return to you individually, and through you, to your society collectively in the United States, my thanks for the demonstrations of affection and the expressions of joy, offered in their behalf, on my late appointment. It shall still be my endeavor to manifest by overt acts the purity of my inclinations for promoting the happiness of mankind, as well as the sincerity of my desires to contribute whatever may be in my power towards the preservation of the civil and religious liberties of the

American people. In pursuing this line of conduct, I hope, by the assistance of Divine Providence, not altogether to disappoint the confidence which you have been pleased to repose in me.

It always affords me satisfaction when I find a concurrence in sentiment and practice between all conscientious men in acknowledgments of homage to the great Governor of the Universe, and in professions of support to a just civil government. After mentioning that I trust the people of every denomination who demean themselves as good citizens will have occasion to be convinced that I shall always strive to prove a faithful and impartial patron of genuine, vital religion, I must assure you in particular, that I take in the kindest part the promise you make of presenting your prayers at the throne of grace for me, and that I likewise implore the divine benediction on yourselves and your religious community.[209]

ADDRESS TO BAPTIST CHURCHES

An address was delivered to the General Committee, representing the United Baptist Churches in Virginia, in May, 1789, as follows:

Gentlemen: I request that you will accept my best acknowledgments for your congratulation on my appointment to the first office in the nation. The kind manner in which you mention my past conduct equally claims the expression of my gratitude.

After we had, by the smiles of Heaven on our exertions, obtained the object for which we contended,

A CHRISTIAN PRESIDENT

I retired, at the conclusion of the war, with the idea that my country could have no farther occasion for my services, and with the intention of never entering again into public life; but, when the exigencies of my country seemed to require me once more to engage in public affairs, an honest conviction of duty superseded my former resolution, and became my apology for deviating from the happy plan which I had adopted.

If I could have entertained the slightest apprehension that the constitution framed in the convention where I had the honor to preside might possibly endanger the religious rights of any ecclesiastical society, certainly I would never have placed my signature to it; and, if I could now conceive that the general government might ever be so administered as to render the liberty of conscience insecure, I beg you will be persuaded that no one would be more zealous than myself to establish effectual barriers against the horrors of spiritual tyranny and every species of religious persecution. For you doubtless remember, that I have often expressed my sentiments that every man conducting himself as a good citizen, and being accountable to God alone for his religious opinions, ought to be protected in worshiping the Deity according to the dictates of his own conscience.

While I recollect with satisfaction that the religious society of which you are members have been, throughout America, uniformly and almost unanimously the firm friend to civil liberty, and the per-

GEORGE WASHINGTON THE CHRISTIAN

severing promoters of our glorious Revolution, I cannot hesitate to believe that they will be the faithful supporters of a free, yet efficient general government. Under this pleasing expectation I rejoice to assure them, that they may rely on my best wishes and endeavors to advance their prosperity.

In the meantime, be assured, Gentlemen, that I entertain a proper sense of your fervent supplications to God for my temporal and eternal happiness.[210]

Presbyterian Church Sends Address to Washington

The first meeting of the "General Assembly of the Presbyterian Church in the U. S. A.," adopted an address to the President of the United States, on the 26th of May, 1789, and who, no doubt, expressed what they knew of his religious character. It is a splendid testimony to his faith in Christianity:

"But we derive a presage even more flattering from the piety of your character. Public virtue is the most certain means of public felicity, and religion is the surest basis of virtue. We therefore esteem it a peculiar happiness to behold in our Chief Magistrate, a steady, uniform, avowed friend of the Christian religion; who has commenced his administration in rational and exalted sentiments of piety; and who, in his private conduct, adorns the doctrines of the gospel of Christ; and on the most public and solemn occasions, devoutly acknowledges the government of Divine Providence."[211]

ADDRESS TO PRESBYTERIAN CHURCH

He delivered the following reply to the address of the General Assembly of the Presbyterian Church in the United States of America, in May, 1789:

Gentlemen: I receive with great sensibility the testimonial given by the General Assembly of the Presbyterian Church in the United States of America, of the lively and unfeigned pleasure experienced by them on my appointment to the first office of the nation.

Although it will be my endeavor to avoid being elated by the too favorable opinion which your kindness for me may have induced you to express of the importance of my former conduct and the effect of my future services, yet, conscious of the disinterestedness of my motives, it is not necessary for me to conceal the satisfaction I have felt upon finding that my compliance with the call of my country and my dependence on the assistance of Heaven to support me in my arduous undertakings have, so far as I can learn, met the universal approbation of my countrymen.

While I reiterate the professions of my dependence upon Heaven as the source of all public and private blessings, I will observe that the general prevalence of piety, philanthropy, honesty, industry, and economy seems, in the ordinary course of human affairs, particularly necessary for advancing and confirming the happiness of our country. While all men within our territories are protected in worshiping the Deity according to the dictates of their consciences, it is rationally to be expected from them in return that they will all be emulous of evincing the sanctity of their professions, of the innocence of their lives, and the beneficence of their actions; for no man who is profligate in his morals, or a bad member of the civil community, can possibly be a true Christian or a credit to his own religious society.

I desire you to accept my acknowledgments for your laudable endeavors to render men sober, honest, and good citizens, and the obedient subjects of a lawful government, as well as for your prayers to Almighty God for His blessings on our common country, and the humble instrument which He has been pleased to make use of in the administration of its government.[212]

Address to the United Brethren

The following address was given to the Directors of the Society of the United Brethren for Propagating the Gospel among the Heathen, in July, 1789:

Gentlemen: I receive with satisfaction the congratulations of your society, and of the Brethren's congregations in the United States of America. For you may be persuaded that the approbation and good wishes of such a peaceable and virtuous community cannot be indifferent to me.

You will also be pleased to accept my thanks for the treatise you presented, ("An account of the manner in which the Protestant Church of the Unitas Fratrum, or United Brethren, preach the Gospel and carry on their mission among the Heathen,") and be assured of my patronage in your laudable undertakings.

In proportion as the general government of the United States shall acquire strength by duration, it is probable they may have it in their power to extend a salutary influence to the aborigines in the extremities of their territory. In the meantime it will be a desirable thing, for the protection of the Union, to cooperate, as far as the circumstances may conveniently admit, with the disinterested endeavors of your Society to civilize and Christianize the savages of the wilderness.

Under these impressions, I pray Almighty God to have you always in his Holy keeping.[213]

ADDRESS TO PROTESTANT EPISCOPAL CHURCH

An address to the Bishops, Clergy, and Laity of the Protestant Episcopal Church in the States of New York, New Jersey, Pennsylvania, Delaware, Maryland, Virginia and North Carolina, in General Convention Assembled, August 19, 1789, is as follows:

Gentlemen: I sincerely thank you for your affectionate congratulations on my election to the chief magistracy of the United States.

After having received from my fellow-citizens in general the most liberal treatment, after having found them disposed to contemplate, in the most flattering point of view, the performance of my military services, and the manner of my retirement at the close of the war, I feel that I have a right to console myself in my present arduous undertakings with a hope that they will still be inclined to put the most favorable construction on the motives which may influence me in my future public transactions.

The satisfaction arising from the indulgent opinion entertained by the American people of my conduct will, I trust, be some security for preventing me from doing anything which might justly incur the forfeiture of that opinion. And the consideration that human happiness and moral duty are inseparably connected, will always continue to prompt me to promote the progress of the former by inculcating the practice of the latter.

On this occasion it would ill become me to conceal the joy I have felt in perceiving the fraternal affection which appears to increase every day among the friends of genuine religion. It affords edifying prospects, indeed, to see Christians of different denominations dwell together in more charity, and conduct themselves in respect to each other with a more Christian-like spirit, than ever they have done in any former age, or in any other nation.

I receive with the greater satisfaction your con-

gratulations on the establishment of the new constitution of government, because I believe its mild
yet efficient operations will tend to remove every
remaining apprehension of those with whose opinions
it may not entirely coincide, as well as to confirm the
hopes of its numerous friends; and because the mod-
eration, patriotism, and wisdom of the present federal Legislature seem to promise the restoration of
order and our ancient virtues, the extension of genuine religion, and the consequent advancement of our
respectability abroad, and of our substantial happiness at home.

I request, most reverend and respected Gentlemen,
that you will accept my cordial thanks for your devout supplications to the Supreme Ruler of the Universe in behalf of me. May you, and the people
whom you represent, be the happy subjects of the
divine benedictions both here and hereafter.[214]

SICKNESS

Soon after his inauguration Washington,
wearied by labor and excitement, was seized
with a violent illness which lasted for six weeks.
One day, being alone with Dr. Samuel Bard, his
physician, he requested to be told, without hesitation, what would be the probable result of this
dangerous attack, saying, "Do not flatter me
with vain hopes; I am not afraid to die, and
therefore can bear the worst."

The doctor's answer, while it expressed hope,
acknowledged his apprehensions. The Presi-

dent replied, "Whether to-night, or twenty years hence, makes no difference; I know that I am in the hands of a good Providence."[215]

DEATH OF HIS MOTHER

Before the President had entirely recovered he received intelligence of the death of his mother on the 25th of August, 1789, at the age of eighty-two.

The following extract from a letter, written by General Washington to his only sister, Mrs. Betty Lewis, of Fredericksburg, Virginia, will attest the filial sensibility with which he regarded the death of his mother, and the pious resignation cherished by him in reference to the event:

Awful and affecting as the death of a parent is, there is consolation in knowing that Heaven has spared ours to an age beyond which few attain, and favored her with the full enjoyment of her mental faculties, and as much bodily strength as usually falls to the lot of fourscore. Under these considerations, and the hope that she is translated to a happier place, it is the duty of her relatives to yield due submission to the decrees of the Creator. When I was last at Fredericksburg I took a final leave of my mother, never expecting to see her more.[216]

FIRST NATIONAL THANKSGIVING

The proclamation for the first national thanksgiving day in the new republic was issued October 3, 1789, as follows:

Whereas, it is the duty of all nations to acknowledge the Providence of Almighty God, to obey his will, to be grateful for his benefits, and humbly to implore his protection and favor; and, whereas, both Houses of Congress have, by their joint committee, requested me "to recommend to the people of the United States a day of public thanksgiving and prayer, to be observed by acknowledging with grateful hearts the many and signal favors of Almighty God, especially by affording them an opportunity peaceably to establish a form of government for their safety and happiness;"

Now, therefore, I do recommend and assign Thursday, the twenty-sixth day of November next, to be devoted by the people of these States to the service of that great and glorious Being, who is the Beneficent Author of all the good that was, that is, or that will be; that we may then all unite in rendering unto Him our sincere and humble thanks for His kind care and protection of the people of this country, previous to their becoming a nation; for the signal and manifold mercies, and the favorable interpositions of His providence, in the course and conclusion of the late war; for the great degree of tranquillity, union, and plenty, which we have since enjoyed; for the peaceable and rational manner in which we have been enabled to establish constitutions of government for our safety and happiness, and particularly the national one now lately instituted; for the civil and religious liberty with which we are blessed, and the means we have of acquiring and diffusing useful knowledge; and, in general, for all the great and various favors, which He has been pleased to confer upon us.

And, also, that we may then unite in most humbly offering our prayers and supplications to the great Lord and Ruler of Nations, and beseech Him to pardon our national and other transgressions; to enable us all, whether in public or private stations, to perform our several and relative duties properly and punctually; to render our national government a blessing to all the people, by constantly being a government of wise, just, and constitutional laws, discreetly and faithfully executed and obeyed; to protect and guide all sovereigns and nations (especially such as have shown kindness to us), and to bless them with good governments, peace, and concord; to promote the knowledge and practice of true religion and virtue, and the increase of science, among them and us; and, generally, to grant unto all mankind such a degree of temporal prosperity as He alone knows to be best.

Given under my hand, at the city of New York, the third day of October, in the year of our Lord one thousand seven hundred and eighty-nine.[217]

CHAPTER XIII
HOW WASHINGTON SPENT SUNDAY
Sundays Away from Home

As soon as his health was restored, after the severe attack we have mentioned, in the first year of his presidency, President Washington made a long-intended tour by carriage through the New England States, traveling in his own chariot, attended on horseback by his secretaries. The following extracts from his diary show how he spent the Sundays away from home, including the last two Sundays at home in New York:

October, 1789
Sunday, 4th

Went to St. Paul's Chappel in forenoon.

Sunday, 11th

At home all day—writing private letters.

Thursday, 15th

Commenced my journey about 9 o'clock for Boston and tour through the Eastern States.

At New Haven, Connecticut
Sunday, 18th [October]

Went in the forenoon to the Episcopal Church, and

in the afternoon to one of the Congregational Meet-ing-Houses.[218]

At Boston, Massachusetts
Sunday, 25th [October]

Attended Divine Service at the Episcopal Church, whereof Doctor Samuel Parker is the Incumbent, in the forenoon, and the Congregational Church of Mr. Thatcher [Rev. Peter Thatcher] in the afternoon.[219]

At Portsmouth, New Hampshire
November 1st, 1789

I went in the forenoon to the Episcopal Church, under the incumbency of a Mr. Ogden; in the after-noon to one of the Presbyterian or Congregational Churches, in which a Mr. Buckminster [Rev. Joseph Buckminster] preached.[220]   (See p. 178.)

A Sunday in Connecticut
Sunday, 8th [November]

It being contrary to law and disagreeable to the People of this State [Connecticut] to travel on the Sabbath Day—and my horses, after passing through such intolerable roads, wanting to rest, I stayed at Perkins' tavern (which, by the by, is not a good one) all day—and a meeting-house being within a few rods of the door, I attended morning and evening service, and heard very lame discourses from a Mr. Pond [Rev. Enoch Pond].[221]

Halted by Officer

On this Sunday, Washington came near being

arrested, as related in the following very interesting incident:

"In the town of ————, in Connecticut, where the roads were extremely rough, Washington was overtaken by night, on Saturday, not being able to reach the town, where he designed to rest on the Sabbath. Next morning about sunrise, his coach was harnessed, and he was proceeding onward to an inn, near the place of worship, which he proposed to attend.

"A plain man, who was an informing officer, came from a cottage, and inquired of the coachman whther there were any urgent reasons for his traveling on the Lord's Day. The General, instead of resenting this as impertinent rudeness, ordered the coachman to stop, and with great civility explained the circumstances to the officer, commending him for his fidelity, and assured him that nothing was farther from his intention than to treat with disrespect the laws and usages of Connecticut, relative to the Sabbath, which met with his most cordial approbation."[222]

Sundays at Home

How Washington spent his Sundays at home in New York, as shown by a few extracts from his diary:

Sunday, 15th [November, 1789]

Went to St. Paul's Chapel in the forenoon.

Sunday, 22nd

Went to St. Paul's Chapel in the forenoon—heard a charity sermon for the benefit of the Orphan's School of this city.

Thursday, 26th

Being the day appointed for a thanksgiving, I went to St. Paul's Chapel, though it was most inclement and stormy—but few people at church.

Sunday, 29th

Went to St. Paul's Chapel in the forenoon.[223]

December, 1789

Sunday, 6th

Went to St. Paul's Chapel in the forenoon.

Sunday, 13th

Went to St. Paul's Chapel in the forenoon.

Sunday, 20th

Went to St. Paul's Chapel in the forenoon.[224]

LETTER TO REV. JOSEPH BUCKMINSTER

The following letter was written from New York, December 23, 1789, to Rev. Joseph Buckminster, D.D., of Portsmouth, New Hampshire, whose church Washington attended November 1, 1789, during his New England trip (see page 176):

Your letter of the 27th of November and the discourse which it enclosed has been duly read. I consider the sermon on the death of Sir William Pepperell, which you were so good as to send me by the desire of Lady Pepperell, his relict, as a mark of attention from her which required my particular acknowledgements; and I am sorry that the death of that lady, which I see announced in the public papers, prevents my thanks being returned to her for her respect and good wishes. You, sir, will please accept them for yourself in forwarding the discourse, and my request that they may be added to the Reverend Clark with my approbation of the doctrine therein inculcated.

This letter to Doctor Buckminster is especially notable, because, though the larger part was dictated, Washington has added in his own hand his "approbation of the doctrine" of the discourse. It is doubtful if in all his writings similar approval of any statement of doctrine can be found. The title of the able discourse alluded to is "A Sermon occasioned by the death of the Honorable Sir William Pepperell, Bart., Lieutenant General in His Majesty's Service, etc., who died at his seat in Kittery (near Portsmouth, N. H.), July 6, 1759; Preached the next Lord's Day after his funeral by Benjamin Stevens, A. M., Pastor of the First Church in Kittery, Boston, etc., 1759."

The text selected for this most eminent per-

sonage of Maine—the only native of America
ever baroneted, though two were knighted
(Fitch and Randolph)—was from the 82d psalm,
"But ye shall die like men" (v. 7.) Referring
to the previous verse, "I have said, Ye are gods,"
the preacher said that rulers might in a sense
be properly so styled, because government being
appointed of God, magistrates were his representatives. He defined God as a moral Governor, engaged in a great plan of wisdom and
benevolence. "As this world is not a state of
Retribution, it is requisite that these earthly
Gods should be removed by Death as well as
other Men, in order to complete the Plan of the
Divine Government. Indeed, the great ends
of the moral administration of God seem to
require this, to suppress the progress of vice and
promote virtue and goodness in the present
state, but especially for the final adjustment of
all things with equity."[225]

DIARY (CONTINUED)

Friday, 25th—*Christmas Day*

Went to St. Paul's Chapel in the forenoon.

Sunday, 27th

At home—all day—weather being bad.

January, 1790

Sunday, 3d

Went to St. Paul's Chapel.

HOW WASHINGTON SPENT SUNDAY

Sunday, 10th
Went to St. Paul's Chapel in the forenoon.

Sunday, 17th
At home all day—not well.

Sunday, 24th
Went to St. Paul's Chapel in the forenoon.

Sunday, 31st
Went to St. Paul's Chapel in the forenoon.

February, 1790
Sunday, 7th
Went to St. Paul's Chapel in the forenoon.

Sunday, 14th
At home all day. Writing private letters to Virginia.

Sunday, 21st
Went to St. Paul's Chapel in the forenoon.

Sunday, 28th
Went to St. Paul's Chapel in the forenoon.

March, 1790
Sunday, 7th
At home all day—writing letters on private business.

Sunday, 14th
Went to St. Paul's Chapel in the forenoon—wrote letters on private business afterwards.

Sunday, 21st

Went to St. Paul's Chapel in the forenoon—wrote private letters in the afternoon.

Received Mr. Jefferson, Minister of State, about one o'clock.

Sunday, 28th

Went to St. Paul's Chapel in the forenoon.[226]

CONSECRATION OF TRINITY CHURCH

Wednesday, March 24, 1790, the new Trinity Church, New York, was consecrated; Bishop Samuel Provoost officiated. The President, Mrs. Washington, and their two children occupied a handsomely draped pew, which the wardens, John Jay and James Duane, had selected and arranged for the Executive family.[227]

DIARY (CONTINUED)

It will be observed that hereafter he attends the new Trinity Church.

April, 1790

Sunday, 4th

At home all day—unwell.

Sunday, 11th

Went to Trinity Church in the forenoon, and wrote several private letters in the afternoon.

Sunday, 18th

At home all day—the weather being very stormy & bad, wrote private letters.

Sunday, 25th

Went to Trinity Church, and wrote letters home after dinner.[228]

May, 1790
Sunday, 2d

Went to Trinity Church in the forenoon—writing letters on private business in the afternoon.

Sunday, 9th

Indisposed with a bad cold, and at home all day writing letters on private business.

June, 1790
Sunday, 27th

Went to Trinity Church in the forenoon—and employed myself in writing business in the afternoon.

July, 1790
Sunday, 4th

Went to Trinity Church in the forenoon. This day being the Anniversary of the Declaration of Independency the celebration of it was put off until to-morrow.

Monday, 5th

About one o'clock a sensible oration was delivered in St. Paul's Chapel by Rev. Brockholst Levingston, on the occasion of the day.

Sunday, 11th

At home all day—dispatching some business relative to my own private concerns.[229]

GEORGE WASHINGTON THE CHRISTIAN

By the extracts from his diary, which we have
quoted, it is seen that during the seven and a
third months, from October 1 to May 9, of
the thirty-two Sundays, Washington attended
church on twenty-five of them. He also attended three times on week days, making twenty-
eight times in all. He remained at home seven
Sundays—three because he was not well, and
two on account of stormy weather; the other
two, apparently, because it was necessary to
attend to private correspondence. Washington
considered that his time during the week belonged to public business, and, therefore, was
obliged to attend to private matters on Sunday.
It will be noticed from his diary that, after Sunday, May 2, he did not attend church again for
several weeks. He states that he became very
ill on May 10 and was convalescent for several
weeks, during which time his diary was suspended. As soon as he is able, he is again found
in his place of worship on the last Sunday in June.

No Sunday Visiting

Though he had, as we have seen, paid a
marked respect to the claims of the Sabbath
throughout his previous life, there seemed to be,
during his Presidency, an increased regard and
deference for the same. Not only was he most
punctual in his attendance on the public worship

of God, whenever it was possible, but the discipline of his house was strictly conformed to the obligations and proprieties of the day. It was an established rule of his mansion that visitors could not be admitted on Sundays. It is understood that an exception to the rule was made in the case of one individual, namely, Mr. Trumbull, speaker of the House of Representatives. He often spent an hour on Sunday evenings with the President; and so entirely was the privilege confined to him that it was usual with the house servant when he heard the door-bell ring, on those evenings, to call it the "Speaker's bell."

After spending a part of the day at church, and occasionally an hour in the evening with Mr. Trumbull, one of the most pious men of his age, the rest of the time preceding the hour of repose was occupied, as previously mentioned, by the President's reading to Mrs. Washington a sermon or a portion of the Holy Scriptures.[230]

CHURCH SUBSCRIPTIONS

November 20, 1790, President Washington reminded his manager at Mount Vernon that on Monday the annual church subscriptions were due, mentioning among other items, ten pounds to the Rev. Thomas Davis, rector of Christ Church, Alexandria.[231]

GEORGE WASHINGTON THE CHRISTIAN

Church Attendance in New York

While he resided in New York, Washington was a regular worshiper at St. Paul's Chapel and Trinity Episcopal Church, and he highly esteemed Bishop Provoost, the rector of Trinity parish, not only as a clergyman, but because he had taken such a bold stand for his country during the Revolution.

CHAPTER XIV

WASHINGTON A COMMUNICANT

THE President was not only a regular attendant at church, but he was a communicant. This fact is conclusively established by the following creditable evidence:

(1) STATEMENT BY DR. CHAPMAN

The following extract is from a volume of sermons published in 1836 by the Rev. George Thomas Chapman, D.D. It is here given because of the authenticity and conclusiveness of the testimony furnished by it:

"He [George Washington] lived at a period when there were less verbal pretensions on the subject of religion, than have become exceedingly fashionable in modern times, and the consequence is that in his life we have more of the substance than the parade of piety. Still he was an open and avowed follower of the Lord of glory. From the lips of a lady of undoubted veracity, yet living [1835] and a worthy communicant of the church, I received the interesting fact that soon after the close of the Revolutionary War *she saw him* partake of the conse-

187

crated symbols of the body and blood of Christ, in Trinity Church, in the city of New York."[232]

(2) TESTIMONY OF MAJOR POPHAM

Further direct testimony is given by Major Popham, a competent witness, as shown by the following extract from a letter of the Rev. Dr. Berrian, of New York, to Mrs. Jane Washington, of Mount Vernon, in answer to some inquiries about General Washington during his residence in New York as President of the United States:

"About a fortnight since I was administering the communion to a sick daughter of Major Popham, and, after the service was over, happening to speak on this subject, I was greatly rejoiced to obtain the information which you so earnestly desired.

"Major Popham served under General Washington during the Revolutionary War, and I believe he was brought as near to him as their difference of rank would admit, being himself a man of great respectability, and connected by marriage with the Morrises, one of the first families in the country. He has still an erect and military air, and a body but little broken at his advanced age. His memory does not seem to be impaired nor his mind to be enfeebled."[233]

"To the above," says Bishop Meade, of the Episcopal Church, "I can add my own testimony, having in different ways become acquainted with the character of Major Popham, and having visited him about the same time mentioned by Dr. Berrian."

(3) EXTRACT FROM MAJOR POPHAM'S LETTER
       TO MRS. JANE WASHINGTON

NEW YORK, March 14, 1839.

MY DEAR MADAM: You will doubtless be not a little surprised at receiving a letter from an individual whose name may possibly never have reached you; but an accidental circumstance has given me the extreme pleasure of introducing myself to your notice. In a conversation with the Reverend Doctor Berrian, a few days since, he informed me that he had lately paid a visit to Mount Vernon, and that Mrs. Washington had expressed a wish to have a doubt removed from her mind, which had long oppressed her, as to the certainty of the General's having attended the communion while residing in the city of New York subsequent to the Revolution. As nearly all the remnants of those days are now sleeping with their fathers, it is not very probable that at this late day an individual can be found who could satisfy this pious wish of your virtuous heart except the writer. It was my great good fortune to have attended St. Paul's Church in this city with the General during the whole period of his residence in New York as President of the United States. The pew of Chief-Justice Morris was situated next to that of the President, close to whom I constantly sat in

Judge Morris's pew, and I am as confident as a memory now laboring under the pressure of fourscore years and seven can make me, that the President had more than once—I believe I may say often—attended at the sacramental table, at which I had the privilege and happiness to kneel with him. And I am aided in my associations by my elder daughter, who distinctly recollects her grandmamma—Mrs. Morris—often mentioned that fact with great pleasure. Indeed, I am further confirmed in my assurance by the perfect recollection of the President's uniform deportment during divine service in church. The steady seriousness of his manner, the solemn, audible, and subdued tone of voice in which he read and repeated the responses, the Chrisitan humility which overspread and adorned the native dignity of the saviour of his country, at once exhibited him a pattern to all who had the honor of access to him. It was my good fortune, my dear madam, to have had frequent intercourse with him. It was my pride and boast to have seen him in various situations—in the flush of victory, in the field, and in the tent—in the church and at the altar, always himself, ever the same.[234]

Church Attendance in Philadelphia

(1) *Testimony of Reverend E. C. M'Guire*

"In December, 1790, Congress met at Philadelphia, and the President, of course, removed there [August 30, 1790]. His conduct continued to be distinguished by the same uniform and punctual observance of religious duties which has always marked his life. He had a pew in Christ Church of that city, of which the venerable Bishop White was then the rector. During all the time that he was in the government Washington was punctual in his attendance on divine worship. His pew was seldom vacant when the weather would permit him to attend."[235]

(2) *Testimony of George Washington Parke Custis*

In regard to his habit at that time (writes the Rev. E. C. M'Guire, in 1835), the living grandson of Mrs. Washington, Geo. W. P. Custis, Esq., of Arlington, Virginia, bears the following testimony: "On Sundays, unless the weather was uncommonly severe, the President and Mrs. Washington attended divine service at Christ Church; and in the evenings the President read to Mrs. Washington, in her chamber, a sermon, or some portion from the Sacred Writings. No visitors, with the exception of Mr. Speaker Trumbull, were admitted to the president's house on Sundays."[236]

(3) *Statement of Bishop White*

The Reverend William White, D.D., bishop of the Protestant Episcopal Church in the Com-

monwealth of Pennsylvania, was the rector of
Christ Church when Washington resided in
Philadelphia. In a letter to the Rev. B. B. C.
Parker, November 28, 1832, he says: "The
father of our country, as well during the Revolutionary War as in his Presidency, attended divine
service in Christ Church in this city [Phila-
delphia] except during one winter (1781-82),
when, being here for the taking of measures with
Congress towards the opening of the next campaign, he rented a house near St. Peter's Church,
then in parochial union with Christ Church.
During that season he attended regularly at
St. Peter's. His behavior was always serious and
attentive; but as your letter seems to intend an
inquiry on the point of kneeling during service, I
owe it to the truth to declare, that I never saw
him in that attitude. During his Presidency
our vestry provided him with a pew not ten
yards in front of the desk. It was habitually
occupied by himself, by Mrs. Washington, who
was regularly a communicant, and by his secretaries."[237]

The fact that Dr. White never saw Washington kneel is of little consequence. The
testimony of other worshipers is that he did
kneel. A minister seldom knows the posture
of individuals in his congregation during
prayer.

(4) *Washington at Church*

"My next view of him was a nearer and more distinct one—it was as a worshiper. My parents, who were Episcopalians, had a front pew in the gallery of Christ Church, in Philadelphia; and from that favorable post of observation I noticed, in the middle aisle, a pew lined with crimson velvet fringed with gold, into which I saw a highly dignified gentleman enter, accompanied by two others, younger than himself, and most respectful in their deportment towards him. These as I have since learned, were members of his military family. I was but a young boy, and the impression, as I well remember, on my youthful mind was, that I had never seen so grand a gentleman before. Everybody else seemed to be of the same mind; for I do not consider it a slander on the very respectable congregation worshiping in that church to say that far more looks were fixed upon that pew than on the pulpit (unless, indeed, it happened to be occupied by that most excellent and venerable of prelates, Bishop White). The deportment of Washington was reverent and attentive; his eyes, when not on the prayer-book, were on the officiating clergyman, and no witless or irreverent worshiper could plead Washington's example. I have since been in the church at Alexandria, in Virginia, which was his parish church—have handled the prayer-book he used, and seen his well-known autograph in front of his Bible; and here the same impression existed as to his regular and exemplary attendance and demeanor. He could not always be present in the church at Philadelphia, in the afternoon, being pressed by the exigency of public affairs, which, in the mind of Washington, were ever held to be matters of necessity. Hence he gave orders that in case certain important despatches were received during his attendance in church, they should be brought to him there; and I have seen them delivered into his hands. He opened them immediately, and deliberately and attentively read them through; then laying them on the seat by his side, he resumed his prayer-book, and, apparently, gave his mind to the solemnities of the place and the hour."[238]

(5) *Takes Communion*

General Robert Porterfield, of Augusta, Georgia, was brigade-inspector under General Washington in the Revolution. His duties brought him in close contact with Washington. General S. H. Lewis, of Augusta County, Georgia, in a letter to the Rev. Mr. Dana, of Alexandria, Virginia, December 14, 1855, says that General Porterfield said to him:

"General Washington was a pious man, and a member of your church [Episcopal]. I saw him myself on his knees receive the sacrament of the Lord's Supper in ——— Church, in Philadelphia.

"He specified the time and place. My impression is that Christ Church was the place, and Bishop White, as he afterward was, the minister. This is, to the best of my recollection, an accurate statement of what I heard from General Porterfield on the subject."[239]

(6) *Withdraws from Communion*

"It is certainly a fact," says Bishop Meade, of the Episcopal Church, "that for a certain period of time during his Presidential term, while Congress was held in Philadelphia, he did not commune. This fact rests on the authority of Bishop White, under whose ministry the President sat, and who was on the most intimate terms with himself and Mrs. Washington. I will relate what the Bishop told myself and others in relation to it. During the session or sessions of Congress held in Philadelphia, General Washington was, with his family, a regular attendant at one of the churches under the care of Bishop White and his assistants. On communion days, when the congregation was dismissed (except the portion which communed), the General left

195

the church, until a certain Sabbath on which
Dr. Abercrombie, in his sermon, spoke of the
impropriety of turning our backs on the Lord's
table, that is, neglecting to commune; from
which time General Washington came no more
on communion days. Bishop White supposes
that the General understood the words 'turning
our backs on the Lord's table' in a somewhat
different sense than was designed by the
preacher; that he supposed it was intended to
censure those who left the church at the time of
its administration, and in order not to seem to
be disrespectful to that ordinance, thought it
better not to be present at all on such occasions.
It is needless to attempt to conjecture what may
have been the reason of this temporary suspension of the act of communicating. A regard for
historic truth has led to the mention of this subject. The question as to his ever having been a
communicant has been raised on this fact, as
stated by Bishop White, and we have thought it
best to give the narrative as we heard it from
the lips of the Bishop himself."[240]

(7) *Bishop Meade's Comment*

Referring to the foregoing statement of Bishop
White, and the fact of Washington's withdrawing
from the communion, Bishop Meade says: "He
may have communed in Philadelphia on some

occasion and yet not been seen by Bishop White, who had the care of two or three churches, at which he officiated alternately in conjunction with one or more ministers. He may have retired, and doubtelss did, at other times, and was seen by Bishop White. If it be asked how we can reconcile this leaving of the church at any time of the celebration of the Lord's Supper with a religious character, we reply by stating a well-known fact, viz.: that in former days there was a most mistaken notion, too prevalent both in England and America, that it was not so necessary in the professors of religion to communicate at all times, but that in this respect persons might be regulated by their feelings, and perhaps by the circumstances in which they were placed. I have had occasion to see much of this in my researches into the habits of the members of the old Church of Virginia. Into this error of opinion and practice General Washington may have fallen, especially at a time when he was peculiarly engaged with the cares of government and a multiplicity of engagements, and when his piety may have suffered some loss thereby."[241]

PRIVATE PRAYER

During his residence in Philadelphia, as President of the United States, it was the habit of Washington, winter and summer, to retire to his study at a certain hour every night. He usually did so at nine o'clock—always having a lighted candle in his hand, and closing the door carefully after him. A youthful member of the household whose room was near the study, being just across the passage, observing this constant practice of the President, had his thoughts excited in reference to the cause of so uniform a custom. Accordingly, on one occasion, in the indulgence of a juvenile curiosity, he looked into the room, some time after the President had gone in; and to his surprise, saw him upon his knees at a small table, with a candle and open Bible thereon.

In these facts we have all the evidence we could ask of his uniform attention to the divinely commanded observance of private prayer. The evidence too embraces a very large portion of his life. Our limited and partial information comprehends a period of forty years—that is, from his twenty-third to beyond his sixtieth year. It was his habit while engaged in the French and Indian war; it was so also during the Revolutionary War; and it was the same during his Presidential terms, and no doubt it was so to the end of his life.[242]

ASKED BLESSING AT TABLE

He was in the habit of asking the divine blessing at his table, although, when a minister of the gospel was present, he requested him to officiate. The late venerable Dr. Ashabel Green, who was one of the chaplains of Congress from 1792 to 1800, says, "It was the usage under President Washington's administration, that the chaplains of Congress should dine with him once in every month, when Congress was in session." He mentions, "that the place of the chaplain was directly opposite to the President. The company stood while the blessing was asked, and on a certain occasion, the President's mind was probably occupied with some interesting concern, and on going to the table he began to ask a blessing himself. He uttered but a word or two, when, bowing to me," says Dr. Green, "he requested me to proceed, which I accordingly did. I mention this," he continues, "because it shows that President Washington always asked a blessing himself when a chaplain was not present."[243]

In some reminiscences of Washington by the Rev. Ashabel Green, we learn that "he always, unless a clergyman was present, at his own table, asked a blessing, in a standing posture. If a clergyman was present, he was requested both to ask a blessing and to return thanks after dinner."[244]

TEMPERANCE
(1) *His Personal Habits*
The "Temperance Cause," as such, had never

been heard of in Washington's day, yet he was strictly temperate. "Not only was he addicted to no kind of intemperance, scarcely ever tasting ardent spirits or exceeding two glasses of wine— which was equal to total abstinence in our day— and not using tobacco in any shape, but he used his authority in the army to the utmost to put down swearing, games of chance, and drinking, and irregularities of every kind."[245]

(2) *His Views*

In a letter to one of his overseers, Washington gives emphatic expression of his views regarding the use of intoxicating liquors, as follows:

I shall not close this letter without exhorting you to refrain from spirituous liquors; they will prove your ruin if you do not. Consider how little a drunken man differs from a beast; the latter is not endowed with reason, the former deprives himself of it; and when that is the case, acts like a brute, annoying and disturbing every one around him; nor is this all, nor, as it respects himself, the worst of it. By degrees it renders a person feeble, and not only unable to serve others but to help himself; and being an act of his own, he falls from a state of usefulness into contempt, and at length suffers, if not perishes, in penury and want.

Don't let this be your case. Show yourself more of a man and a Christian than to yield to so intolerable a vice, which cannot, I am certain (to the greatest

WASHINGTON A COMMUNICANT

lover of liquor), give more pleasure to sip in the poison (for it is no better) than the consequence of it in bad behavior at the moment, and the more serious evils produced by it afterwards, must give pain.

I am your Friend,
GEORGE WASHINGTON.[246]

ATTENDS DUTCH REFORMED CHURCH

In his diary we find the following for Sunday, July 3, 1791, at Lancaster, Pennsylvania:

"There being no Episcopal minister *present* in this place, I went to hear morning service performed in the Dutch Reformed Church—which, being in that language not a word of which I understood, I was in no danger of becoming a proselyte to its religion by the eloquence of the preacher."[247]

LETTER TO LaFAYETTE

Writing to the Marquis LaFayette, July 28, 1791, concerning the revolutionary troubles in France, he says, "We must, however, place a confidence in that Providence who rules events, trusting that out of confusion He will produce order, and, notwithstanding the dark clouds which may threaten at present, that right will ultimately be established."[248]

ON THE DEATH OF A CHILD

September 8, 1791, President Washington

Age 59]   201   [1791

wrote to General and Mrs. Knox on the death of their child, who had been named for him. On this occasion, as on every other when opportunity offered, he gave assurance of his abiding faith in God. He said: "He that gave, you know, has the right to take way. His ways are wise—they are inscrutable—and irresistible."[249]

CHAPTER XV

DID WASHINGTON SWEAR?

In relation to what is sometimes said about the paroxysms of passion and terrible swearing of General Washington, a complete account of the particular instance which has been so grossly magnified and distorted, is of much interest. It was when Washington received the news of General St. Clair's defeat by the Indians, which occurred November 4, 1791.

(1) Statement by His Private Secretary

The following extract from a synopsis of General Washington's private letters to his secretary, Mr. Tobias Lear, by the Hon. Richard Rush, of Philadelphia, will throw some light on the subject:

"An anecdote I derived from Colonel Lear shortly before his death in 1816 may here be related, showing the height to which his [General Washington's] passion would rise, yet be controlled. It belongs to his domestic life which I am dealing with, having occurred under his own roof, whilst it marks public feeling the most intense and points to the moral of his life.

I give it in Colonel Lear's words as nearly as I can, having made a note of them at the time.

"Toward the close of a winter's day in 1791, an officer in uniform was seen to dismount in front of the President's in Philadelphia, and, giving the bridle to his servant, knock at the door of his mansion. Learning from the porter that the President was at dinner, he said he was on public business and had dispatches for the President. A servant was sent into the dining room to give the information to Mr. Lear, who left the table and went into the hall, when the officer repeated what he had said. Mr. Lear replied that, as the President's secretary, he would take charge of the dispatches and deliver them at the proper time. The officer made answer that he had just arrived from the Western army, and his orders were to deliver it with all promptitude, and to the President in person; but that he would wait his directions. Mr. Lear returned, and in a whisper imparted to the President what had passed. General Washington rose from the table and went to the officer. He was back in a short time, made a word of apology for his absence, but no allusion to the cause of it. He had company that day. Everything went on as usual. Dinner over, the gentlemen passed into the drawing room of Mrs. Washington, which was open in the evening. The General spoke courteously to every lady in the room, as was his custom. His hours were early, and by ten all the company had gone. Mrs. Washington and Mr. Lear remained. Soon Mrs. Washington left the room. The General now walked backward and forward slowly for some minutes without speaking. Then he sat down on a sofa by the fire, telling Mr. Lear to sit down. To this moment there had been no change in his manner since his interruption at table. Mr. Lear now perceived emotion. This rising in him, he broke out suddenly: *'It's all over—St. Clair's defeated, routed; the officers nearly all killed, the men by wholesale; the rout complete— too shocking to think of—and a surprise into the bargain!'*

"He uttered all this with great vehemence, then he paused, got up from the sofa and walked about the room several times, agitated, but saying nothing. Near the door he stopped short and stood still for a few seconds, when his wrath became terrible.

" *'Yes,'* he burst forth, 'HERE, *on this very spot, I took leave of him: I wished him success and honor. "You have your instructions," I said, "from the Secretary of War; I had a strict eye to them, and will add but one word*—BEWARE OF A SURPRISE! *I repeat it,* BEWARE OF A SURPRISE; *you know how the Indians fight us."* He

*went off with that as my last solemn warning
thrown into his ears.   And yet! to suffer that army
to be cut to pieces, hacked, butchered, tomahawked,
by a surprise—the very thing I guarded him
against!   O God, O God, he's worse than a mur-
derer!   How can he answer it to his country? The
blood of the slain is upon him—the curse of the
widows and orphans—the curse of Heaven!'*

"This torrent came out in tones appalling.
His very frame shook.   'It was awful,' said Mr.
Lear.   More than once he threw his hands up as
he hurled imprecations upon St. Clair.   Mr.
Lear remained speechless, awed into breathless
silence.

"The roused chief sat down on the sofa once
more.   He seemed conscious of his passion, and
uncomfortable.   He was silent.   His warmth beginning to subside, he at length said in an altered
voice, 'This must not go beyond this room.'
Another pause followed—a longer one—when
he said in a tone quite low: *'General St. Clair
shall have justice; I looked hastily through the dispatches, saw the whole disaster, but not all the particulars.   I will receive him without displeasure;
I will hear him without prejudice; he shall have
full justice.'*

" 'He was now,' said Mr. Lear, 'perfectly
calm.'   Half an hour had gone by.   The storm
was over; and no sign of it was afterwards seen

in his conduct or heard in his conversation. The whole case was investigated by Congress. St. Clair was exculpated, and regained the confidence Washington had in him when appointing him to that command. He had put himself into the thickest of the fight and escaped unhurt, though so ill as to be carried on a litter, and unable to mount his horse without help."[250]

(2) BISHOP MEADE'S COMMENT

"In relation to the above, let it be granted that Mr. Lear (who did not sympathize with General Washington's religious opinions), after the lapse of more than twenty years, retained an accurate recollection of all his words, and that Mr. Rush fully understood them and truly recorded them, as doubtless he did; yet what do they amount to? Is the exclamation, 'O God! O God!' under his aroused feelings, that swearing since imputed to him, but which from his youth up he had so emphatically condemned in his soldiers as impious and ungentlemanly?"[251]

(3) TESTIMONY OF NEPHEWS

The Rev. Dr. M'Guire of Fredericksburg, Virginia, while preparing his volume on the Religious Opinions and Character of Washington, having heard this report emanating from some of the enemies of Washington and too readily admitted by some of his friends, made a particular inquiry of Mr. Robert Lewis (his father-in-law), of Fredericksburg, and Mr. Laurence Lewis, of Woodlawn, Virginia, two gentlemen as competent to know the private habits of Washington as any others in the land. They were nephews of General Washington. The former lived in the family of Washington for some time as private secretary; the latter was his near neighbor, living on a farm given him by the General. Both of them were men of the highest character, and pious members of the Episcopal Church, and both declared that they had never heard an oath from the lips of their uncle.[252]

(4) Testimony of General Porterfield

In a letter of General S. H. Lewis, referred to on p. 194 telling of a conversation with General Robert Porterfield, he says: "I remarked that I had lately heard Mr. ――― say, on the authority of Mr. ―――, that General Washington was subject to violent fits of passion, and that he swore terribly. General Porterfield said the charge was false; that he had known General Washington personally for many years, and had never heard him swear an oath, or in any way to profane the name of God. 'Tell Mr. ――― for me,' said he, 'that he had much better be reading his Bible than repeating such slanders on the character of General Washington.' "[253]

(5) REBUKES SWEARING

So far back as 1756 we find him endeavoring to impress upon the soldiers under his command a profound reverence for the name and the majesty of God, and repeatedly, in his public orders during the Revolution, the inexcusable offense of profaneness was rebuked.

On a certain occasion he had invited a number of officers to dine with him. While at table one of them uttered an oath. General Washington dropped his knife and fork in a moment, and in his deep undertone, and characteristic dignity and deliberation, said, "I thought that we all supposed ourselves gentlemen." He then resumed his knife and fork and went on as before. The remark struck like an electric shock, and, as was intended, did execution, as his observations in such cases were apt to do. No person swore at the table after that. When dinner was over, the officer referred to said to a companion that if the General had given him a blow over the head with his sword, he could have borne it, but that the home thrust which he received was too much—it was too much for a gentleman![254]

CHAPTER XVI

RELIGION INDISPENSABLE TO POLITICAL PROSPERITY

God Alone Able to Protect United States

Writing from Philadelphia to John Armstrong, March 11, 1792, he says:

I am sure there never was a people who had more reason to acknowledge a divine interposition in their affairs than those of the United States, and I should be pained to believe that they had forgotten that agency, which was so often manifested during our Revolution, or that they failed to consider the omnipotence of that God, who is alone able to protect them.[255]

Trusts God for Guidance

Edmund Randolph, attorney-general, had written Washington, urging him to accept a re-election. Writing from Mount Vernon, Sunday, August 26, 1792, Washington said, "But as the All-wise Disposer of events has hitherto watched over our steps, I trust that, in the important one I may soon be called upon to take, he will mark the course so plainly that I cannot mistake the way."[256]

RELIGION INDISPENSABLE

DEPRECATES RELIGIOUS DISPUTES

Writing from Philadelphia to Sir Edward Newenham, October 20, 1792, he says:

Of all the animosities which have existed among mankind, those which are caused by a difference of sentiments in religion appear to be the most inveterate and distressing, and ought most to be deprecated. I was in hopes that the enlightened and liberal policy which has marked the present age would at least have reconciled *Christians* of every denomination so far that we should never again see their religious disputes carried to such a pitch as to endanger the peace of society.[257]

GIFT TO CHARITY

Following the terrible epidemic of yellow fever, the President wrote to William White, Bishop of Pennsylvania, December 31, 1793, concerning a contribution for the relief of the needy in Philadelphia, as follows:

It has been my intention ever since my return to the city, to contribute my mite towards the relief of the *most* needy inhabitants of it. The pressure of public business hitherto has suspended but not altered my resolution. I am at a loss, however, for whose benefit to apply the little I can give, and in whose hands to place it; whether for the use of the fatherless children and widows, made so by the late calamity, who may find it difficult, whilst provisions, wood, and other necessaries are so dear, to support themselves; or to other and better purposes, if any, I know not, and therefore have taken the liberty of asking your advice.

I persuade myself justice will be done to my motives for giving you this trouble. To obtain information, and to render the little I can, without ostentation or mention of my name, are the sole objects of these inquiries.[258]

Donation for the Education of Orphan Children

February 24, 1794, the President writes to the Rev. James Muir, pastor of the Presbyterian Church at Alexandria, Virginia, in regard to his annual subscription to the Orphan School under the care of Mr. Muir, as follows:

I have received your letter of the 12th instant, and will direct my manager, Mr. Pearce, to pay my annual donation for the education of orphan children, or the children of indigent parents, who are unable to be at the expense themselves.

I had pleasure in appropriating this money to such uses, as I always shall in that of paying it. I confess, however, I should derive satisfaction from knowing what children have heretofore received the benefit of it, and who are now in the enjoyment thereof.

Never, since the commencement of this institution, have I received the least information, except in a single instance, on this head, although application for it to individuals has been frequently made. As you, Sir, appear to be in the exercise of this trust, let me pray you to have the goodness to gratify this wish of mine.

In reply to this letter, Mr. Muir gave a particular account of each of the children who were assisted in their education by President Washington's donation to the school. They were mostly from the poorest class, and some of them entirely destitute of any other aid. For many years he had given fifty pounds (two hundred and fifty dollars) a year for this purpose, which he continued till his death; and by will he left to the trustees of the Academy in the town of Alexandria four thousand dollars, "towards the support of a free school, established at, and annexed to, the said Academy, for the purpose of educating orphan children, or the children of such poor and indigent persons, as are unable to accomplish it by their own means." This sum was bequeathed in perpetuity, and the income only for the time being was to be appropriated by the trustees.[259]

On the same day, February 24, 1794, Washington wrote to his manager, William Pearce, "Enclosed you will find three bank notes of one hundred dollars each; out of which pay the Rev. Mr. Muir, of Alexandria, fifty pounds, and take his signature to the enclosed receipt."[260]

GEORGE WASHINGTON THE CHRISTIAN

GOD KNOWS BEST

In a letter written from Philadelphia to his manager, Mr. William Pearce, on Sunday, May 25, 1794, concerning injury to crops by the drought, he says, "At disappointments and losses which are the effects of Providential acts, I never repine; because I am sure the allwise Disposer of events knows better than we do what is best for us, or what we deserve."[261]

ATTENDS PRESBYTERIAN CHURCH

On a trip to the western part of Pennsylvania in connection with the "Whiskey Rebellion," he spends a Sunday, October 5, 1794, at Carlisle, Pennsylvania. The following entry is found in his diary: "Went to the Presbyterian Meeting and heard Doctor Davidson preach a political sermon, recommendatory of order and good government; and the excellence of that of the United States."[262]

SPEECH TO CONGRESS

He closes a speech to both Houses of Congress, November 19, 1794, saying:

Let us unite, therefore, in imploring the Supreme Ruler of nations to spread His holy protection over these United States; to turn the machinations of the wicked to the confirming of our constitution; to enable us at all times to root out internal sedition, and put invasion to flight; to perpetuate to our country that prosperity, which His goodness has already conferred; and to verify the anticipations of this government being a safeguard to human rights.[263]

SECOND NATIONAL THANKSGIVING

The Proclamation for a second National Thanksgiving was issued January 1, 1795, as follows:

When we review the calamities which afflict so many other nations, the present condition of the United States affords much matter of consolation and satisfaction. Our exemption hitherto from foreign war, and increasing prospect of the continuance of that exemption, the great degree of internal tranquillity we have enjoyed, the recent confirmation of that tranquillity by the suppression of an insurrection, which so wantonly threatened it, the happy course of our public affairs in general, the unexampled prosperity of all classes of our citizens, are circumstances which peculiarly mark our situation with indications of the Divine Beneficence towards us. In such a state of things it is in an especial manner our duty as a people, with devout reverence and affectionate gratitude, to acknowledge our many and great obligations to Almighty God, and to implore Him to continue and confirm the blessings we experience.

Deeply penetrated with this sentiment, I, George Washington, President of the United States, do recommend to all religious societies and denominations, and to all persons whomsoever within the United States, to set apart and observe Thursday, the 19th day of February next, as a day of public thansksgiving and prayer, and on that day to meet together and render their sincere and hearty thanks to the Great Ruler of nations for the manifold and signal mercies which distinguish our lot as a nation; particularly for the possession of constitutions of government, which unite, and by their union establish, liberty with order; for the preservation of our peace, foreign and domestic; for the seasonable control which has been given to a spirit of disorder in the suppression of the late insurrection; and, generally, for the prosperous course of our affairs public and private; and at the same time humbly and fervently to beseech the kind Author of those blessings graciously to prolong them to us; to imprint on our hearts a deep and solemn sense of our obligations to Him for them; to teach us rightly to estimate their immense value; to preserve us from the arrogance of prosperity, and from hazarding the advantages we enjoy by the delusive pursuits, to dispose us to merit the continuance of His favors by not abusing them, by our gratitude for them, and by a correspondent conduct as citizens and as men; to render this country more and more a safe and propitious asylum for the unfortunate of other countries; to extend among us true and useful knowledge; to diffuse and establish habits of sobriety, order, morality, and piety; and finally to impart all the blessings we possess, or ask for ourselves, to the whole family of mankind.

RELIGION INDISPENSABLE

In testimony whereof, I have caused the seal of the United States of America to be affixed to these presents, and signed the same with my hand. Done at the city of Philadelphia, this first day of January, one thousand seven hundred and ninty-five and of the independence of the United States of America the nineteenth.[264]

OBSERVES THANKSGIVING DAY

Thursday, February 19, 1795, being the day appointed for "public thanksgiving and prayer," President Washington attends service in Christ Church.[265]

SPEECH TO CONGRESS

A speech to both Houses of Congress, December 8, 1795, begins as follows:

I trust I do not deceive myself while I indulge the persuasion that I have never met you at any period when, more than at present, the situation of our public affairs has afforded just cause for mutual congratulation, and for inviting you to join with me in profound gratitude to the Author of all good, for the numerous and extraordinary blessings we enjoy.[266]

RELIGION INDISPENSABLE TO POLITICAL PROSPERITY

September 17, 1796, President Washington issued what is known as his Farewell Address to the people of the United States. The following extracts show his deep religious spirit:

Of all the dispositions and habits which lead to political prosperity, Religion and Morality are indispensable supports. In vain would that man claim the tribute of Patriotism, who should labor to subvert these great pillars of human happiness, these firmest props of the duties of Men and Citizens. The mere Politician, equally with the pious man, ought to respect and to cherish them. A volume could not trace all their connections with private and public felicity. Let it simply be asked, Where is the security for property, for reputation, for life, if the sense of religious obligation *desert* the oaths which are the instruments of investigation in Courts of Justice? And let us with caution indulge the supposition that morality can be maintained without religion. Whatever may be conceded to the influence of refined education on minds of peculiar structure, reason and experience both forbid us to expect that national morality can prevail in exclusion of religious principle.

It is substantially true that virtue or morality is a necessary spring of popular government. The rule, indeed, extends with more or less force to every species of free government. Who, that is a sincere friend to it, can look with indifference upon attempts to shake the foundation of the fabric?

. . . .

Observe good faith and justice towards all Nations; cultivate peace and harmony with all. Religion and Morality enjoin this conduct; and can it be that good policy does not equally enjoin it? It will be worthy of a free, enlightened, and, at no distant period, a great Nation, to give to mankind the magnanimous and too novel example of a people always guided by an exalted justice and benevolence. Who can doubt, that, in the course of time and things, the fruits of such a plan would richly repay any temporary advantages, which might be lost by a steady adherence to it? Can it be that Providence has not connected the permanent felicity of a Nation with its Virtue? The experiment, at least, is recommended by every sentiment which ennobles human nature.[267]

The Great High Priest of the Nation

"No candid man can read these and other expressions in the public addresses of Washington, without acknowledging that, as though he were the great high priest of the nation, availing himself of his position and of the confidence reposed in him, he was raising his warning voice against that infidelity which was desolating France and threatening our own land."

"Is is too much to say that the communications of no king, ruler, general, or statesman in Christendom," except Abraham Lincoln, "ever so abounded in expressions of pious dependence on God?"[268]

Letter to Adopted Son in School

Extract from a letter to George Washington

Parke Custis, his adopted son, written from Philadelphia, November 28, 1796, showing the high value he places upon religious obligations:

The assurances you give me of applying diligently to your studies, and fulfilling those obligations which are enjoined by your Creator and due to His creatures, are highly pleasing and satisfactory to me. I rejoice in it on two accounts; first, as it is the sure means of laying the foundation of your own happiness, and rendering you, if it should please God to spare your life, a useful member of society hereafter; and secondly, that I may, if I live to enjoy the pleasure, reflect that I have been, in some degree, instrumental in affecting these purposes.[269]

LAST SPEECH TO CONGRESS

He begins his last speech to both Houses of Congress, December 7, 1796, saying:

In recurring to the internal situation of our country, since I last had the pleasure to address you, I find ample reason for a renewed expression of that gratitude to the Ruler of the Universe, which a continued series of prosperity has so often and so justly called forth.

He closes by saying:

The situation in which I now stand, for the last time, in the midst of the representatives of the people of the United States, naturally recalls the period when the administration of the present form of government commenced; and I cannot omit the occasion to congratulate you and my country, on the success of the experiment, nor to repeat my fervent supplications to the Supreme Ruler of the Universe and Sovereign Arbiter of the United States, that the virtue and happiness of the people may be preserved; and that the government, which they have instituted for the protection of their liberties, may be perpetual.[270]

ANOTHER LETTER TO HIS ADOPTED SON

Writing from Philadelphia to George Washington Parke Custis, December 19, 1796, he emphasizes again "duties to God and man":

But as you are well acquainted with my sentiments on this subject, and you know how anxious all your friends are to see you enter upon the grand theatre of life, with the advantages of a finished education, a highly cultivated mind, and a proper sense of your duties to God and man, I shall only add one sentiment more before I close this letter (which, as I have others to write, will hardly be in time for the mail), and that is, to pay due respect and obedience to your tutors, and affectionate reverence to the president of the college, whose character merits your highest regards.[271]

ADDRESS OF PHILADELPHIA CLERGY

(1) *Written by the Rev. Ashabel Green, D.D.*

"On the 4th of March [1797], when he carried

into effect his purpose of retirement, which he had previously announced, the city clergy waited on him with an address; which, with his answer, was published in the newspapers of the day. Mr. Jefferson, in a letter published after his death, speaks of the design of this address, and of the character of its answer, as indicating that Washington was suspected of infidelity, and broadly intimates that such a suspicion was just. As to the design of the address, I may be allowed to say that Mr. Jefferson's remarks are incorrect, since by the appointment of my clerical brethren, it was penned by myself, and I have not a doubt that the whole imputation is utterly groundless."[272]

(2) *The Address to Washington*

The address shows how the clergy regarded Washington's religious character. It is as follows:

To George Washington, President of the United States:

On this day, which becomes important in the annals of America, as marking the close of a splendid public life devoted for near half a century to the service of your country, we, the undersigned clergy of different denominations residing in and near the city of Philadelphia, beg leave to join the voice of our fellow-citizens, in expressing a deep sense of your public services, in every department of trust and authority committed to you. But in our special character as ministers of the gospel of Christ, we are more immediately bound to acknowledge the countenance which you have uniformly given to His holy religion.

In your public character we have uniformly beheld the edifying example of a civil ruler always acknowledging the superintendence of divine Providence in the affairs of men; and confirming that example by the powerful recommendation of religion and morality, as the firmest basis of social happiness—more especially in the following language of your affectionate parting address to your fellow-citizens:

"Of all the dispositions and habits which lead to political prosperity, religion and morality are indispensable supports. In vain would that man claim the tribute of patriotism who should labor to subvert these great pillars of human happiness, these firmest props of the duties of men and citizens. The mere politician, equally with the pious man, ought to respect and to cherish them. A volume could not trace all their connections with private and public felicity. Let us with caution indulge the supposition that morality can be maintained without religion. Reason and experience both forbid us to expect that national morality can prevail in exclusion of religious principles."

Should the importance of these just and pious sentiments be duly appreciated and regarded, we confidently trust that the prayers you have offered for the prosperity of our common country will be answered. In these prayers we most fervently unite; and with equal fervor we join in those which the numerous public bodies that represent the citizens of these States are offering for their beloved chief. We most devoutly implore the divine blessing to attend you in your retirement, to make it in all respects comfortable to you, to satisfy you with length of days; and finally to receive you into happiness and glory infinitely greater than this world can bestow.[273]

This address was signed by William White (Episcopal bishop), Ashabel Green, and twenty-three other ministers.

(3) *Washington's Reply*

Not to acknowledge, with gratitude and sensibility, the affectionate addresses and benevolent wishes of my fellow-citizens on my retiring from public life would prove that I have been unworthy of the confidence which they have been pleased to repose in me.

And among those public testimonies of attachment and approbation none can be more grateful than that of so respectable a body as yours.

Believing, as I do, that *Religion and Morality are the essential* pillars of civil society, I view with unspeakable pleasure that harmony and brotherly love which characterizes the clergy of different denominations, as well in this as in other parts of the United States, exhibiting to the world a new and interesting spectacle, at once the pride of our country and the surest basis of universal harmony.

That your labors for the good of mankind may be crowned with success, that your temporal employments may be commensurate with your merits, and that the future reward of good and faithful servants may be yours, I shall not cease to supplicate the Divine Author of life and felicity.[274]

CHAPTER XVII

EVEN DOWN TO OLD AGE

Forsakes Not the House of God

Even down to his old age the Sabbath day finds him in his place in church. In his diary is this entry: "1798. Sunday, September 30—Went to Church in Alexandria."[275]

Letter to President Adams

In a letter dated Mount Vernon, July 13, 1798, to John Adams, President of the United States, General Washington said:

Satisfied, therefore, that you have sincerely wished and endeavored to avert war, and exhausted, to the last drop, the cup of reconciliation, we can, with pure hearts, appeal to Heaven for the justice of our cause; and may confidently trust the final result to that kind Providence who has, heretofore, and so often, signally favored the people of these United States.[276]

Will Not Sell Slaves

August 17, 1799, General Washington wrote his nephew Robert Lewis in regard to slavery, saying:

To sell the overplus I cannot because I am prejudiced against this kind of traffic in the human species; to hire them out is almost as bad, because they cannot be disposed of in families to any advantage, and to divide families I have an aversion.[277]

Death of His Brother

Sunday, September 22, 1799, he writes to Colonel Burgess Ball concerning the death of his [Washington's] brother, the last of the family except himself, as follows:

Your letter of the 16th inst. has been received, informing me of the death of my brother [Charles].

The death of relations always produces awful and affecting emotions under whatever circumstances it may happen. That of my brother has been long expected; and his latter days, so uncomfortable to himself, must have prepared all around him for the stroke, though painful in effect.

I was the first, and am, now, the last of my father's children, by the second marriage, who remain.

When I shall be called upon to follow them is known only to the Giver of Life. When the summons comes I shall endeavor to obey it with a good grace.[278]

Attends Christ Church Again

After his retirement from the chair of state, Washington still continued his religious habits in spirit and practice. The church in Alexandria was again his place of worship. The distance, indeed, was ten miles, and yet his pew was seldom unoccupied on the Lord's Day.[279]

WASHINGTON AT CHURCH IN ALEXANDRIA

Reverend M'Guire, Episcopal rector at Fredericksburg, Virginia, says that, many years since [this was written in 1835], he had the following circumstances from a valued female friend, in relation to the churchgoing habit of the Ex-President:

"In the summer of 1799," said Mrs. M., "I was in Alexandria, on a visit to the family of Mr. H., with whom I was connected by the ties of relationship. Whilst there I expressed a wish to see General Washington, as I had never enjoyed that pleasure. My friend, Mrs. H., observed, 'You will certainly see him on Sunday, as he is never absent from church when he can get there; and as he often dines with us, we will ask him on that day, when you will have a better opportunity of seeing him.' Accordingly, we all repaired to church on Sunday, and seated in Mr. H.'s large double pew, I kept my eyes upon the door, looking for the venerable form of him I had so long desired to see. Many persons entered the doors, but none came up to my impressions of General Washington's appearance. At length, a person of noble and majestic figure entered, and the conviction was instantaneous that I beheld the Father of his Country. It was so!—my friend at that moment intimated the fact to me. He walked to his pew, at the upper part of the church, and demeaned himself throughout the services of the day with that gravity and propriety becoming the place and his own high character. After the services were concluded we waited for him at the door, for his pew being near the pulpit he was among the last that came out—when Mrs. H: invited him to dine with us. He declined, however, the invitation, observing, as he looked at the sky, that he thought there were appearances of a thunderstorm in the afternoon, and he believed he would return home for dinner."

This occurrence is introduced, not for any peculiar interest belonging to it, but merely for confirmation: showing the punctuality and conscientiousness with which Washington attended to the duty in question, even to old age. He was now within six months of his death, having reached his sixty-eighth year; and yet he is not to be detained on the Sabbath from the house of God, either by distance or the fervors of a summer sun.[280]

PRIVATE DEVOTIONS

"It may most positively be affirmed that the impression on the minds of his family was that when on each night he regularly took his candle and went to his study at nine o'clock and remained there until ten, it was for the purpose of reading the Scriptures and prayer. It is affirmed by more than one that he has been seen there on his knees and also been heard at his prayers. In like manner it is believed that when at five o'clock each morning, winter and summer, he went to that same study, a portion of time was then spent in the same way. It is also well known that it was the impression in the army that Washington, either in his tent or in his room, practiced the same thing. One testifies to having seen him on more than one occasion thus engaged on his bended knees. It is firmly believed that when in crowded lodgings at Valley Forge, where everything was unfavorable to private devotions, his frequent visits to a neighboring wood were for this purpose. It is also a fact well known to the family that, when prevented from public worship, he used to read the Scriptures and other books with Mrs. Washington in her chamber."[281]

GRACE AT TABLE

Washington's religious habits were the same in private life as when he occupied his official position. The artist, Sharples, who spent some time at Mount Vernon painting Washington's picture, says: "I take all my meals with the Chief at Mount Vernon; they are most elegantly served, but without the least profusion, and the attendance is of military precision. I observed that we never partook of food without the General offering grace to the Giver, so also at the close of every repast."[282]

IMPRESSED BY A DREAM

For several months before his death Washington appears to have had at times a presentiment of near approaching death. July 9th he executed his last will and testament. He seems to have communicated his forebodings to Mrs. Washington, who, when she was recovering from a severe illness, wrote to a kinswoman in New Kent, Virginia, September 18, 1799:

"At midsummer the General had a dream so deeply impressed on his mind that he could not shake it off for several days. He dreamed that he and I were sitting in the summer-house, conversing about the happy life we had spent, and looking forward to many more years on the earth, when suddenly there was a great light all around us, and then an almost invisible figure of a sweet angel stood by my side and whispered in my ear. I suddenly turned pale and then began to vanish from his sight and he was left alone. I had just risen from the bed when he awoke and told me his dream, saying, 'You know a contrary result indicated by dreams may be expected. I may soon leave *you*.' I tried to drive from his mind the sadness that had taken possession of it, by laughing at the absurdity of being disturbed by an idle dream, which, at the worst, indicated that I would *not* be taken from him; but I could not, and it was not until after dinner that he recovered any cheerfulness. I found in the library, a few days afterwards, some scraps of paper which showed that he had been making a Will, and had copied it. When I was so very sick, lately, I thought of this dream, and concluded my time had come, and that I should be taken first."[283]

"I DIE HARD"

About five o'clock [Saturday, December 14, 1799] Dr. Craik [the family physician] came again into the room, and, upon going to the bedside, the General said to him, "Doctor, I die hard, but I am not afraid to go."[284]

"NOT AFRAID TO DIE"

Silent and sad his physicians sat by his bedside, looking on him as he lay panting for breath. They thought on the past, and the tears welled in their eyes. He marked it, and, stretching out his hand to them, and shaking his head, said,

"*O no! don't! don't!*" then with a delightful smile he added, "I am dying, gentlemen, but, thank God, I am not afraid to die."[285]

"For My Good"

Once or twice he was heard to say, "I should have been glad, had it pleased God, to die a little easier, but I doubt not it is for my good."[286]

Wished to Be Left Alone

"Feeling that the hour of his departure out of this world was at hand, he desired that everybody would quit the room. They all went out; and, according to his wish, left him—with his God.

"There, by himself, like Moses alone on the top of Pisgah, he seeks the face of God."[287]

It seems that he desired to be alone a little while for private prayer.

" 'Tis Well"

His secretary, Tobias Lear, says that "about ten o'clock he made several attempts to speak to me before he could effect it. At length he said: 'I am just going. Have me decently buried; and do not let my body be put into the vault in less than three days after I am dead.'

"I bowed assent, for I could not speak. He

then looked at me again and said: 'Do you understand me?'

"I replied, 'Yes!'

"' 'Tis well,' said he."[288]

LAST WORDS OF WASHINGTON

"Feeling that the silver cord of life is loosing, and that his spirit is ready to quit her old companion, the body, he extends himself on his bed —closes his eyes for the last time with his own hands—folds his arms decently on his breast, then breathing out, 'Father of mercies, take me to thyself,'—he falls asleep."[289]

SUBMISSION TO THE DIVINE WILL

"He expired in the sixty-eighth year of his age, and in full possession of his mental faculties; exhibiting in his short and painful illness, and in his death, the same example of patience, fortitude, and submission to the divine will, which he had shown in all the acts of his life."[290]

MRS. WASHINGTON IN PRAYER

Mrs. Washington's grandson, who lived at Mount Vernon, says: "In that last hour, prayer was not wanting at the throne of grace. Close to the couch of the sufferer, resting her head upon that ancient book, with which she had been wont to hold pious communion a portion of every day for more than half a century, was the venerable consort [Mrs. Washington] absorbed in silent prayer."[291]

" 'TIS WELL"

At the moment of her husband's departure, Mrs. Washington, having arisen from her knees, was sitting near the foot of the bed, where she had been much of the time for almost twenty-four hours.

"While we were all fixed in silent grief," wrote Mr. Lear, "Mrs. Washington asked, with a firm and collected voice, 'Is he gone?' I could not speak, but held up my hand as a signal that he was no more. ' 'Tis well,' she said in the same voice; 'all is now over. I shall soon follow him; I have no more trials to pass through.' "[292]

MRS. WASHINGTON'S DAILY DEVOTIONS

Mrs. Washington's grandson, who was adopted by Mr. Washington when he was six months old, and who was in his nineteenth year when Washington died, says of his grandmother's life-long habit: "After breakfast she retired for an hour to her chamber, which hour was spent in prayer and reading the Holy Scriptures, a practice that she never omitted during half a century of her varied life."[293]

DEATH OF MRS. WASHINGTON

Her grandson gives the following account of her death:

"In a little more than two years from the demise of the chief Mrs. Washington became alarmingly ill from an attack of bilious fever. From her advanced age, the sorrow that had preyed upon her spirits, and the severity of the attack, the family physician gave but little hope of a favorable issue. The lady herself was perfectly aware that her hour was nigh; she assembled her grandchildren at her bedside, discoursed to them on their respective duties through life, spoke of the happy influence of religion upon the affairs of this world, of the consolations they had afforded her in many and trying afflictions, and the hopes that they held out of a blessed immortality; and then, surrounded by her weeping relatives, friends, and domestics, the venerable relict of Washington resigned her life into the hands of her Creator, in the seventy-first year of her age."[294]

CHAPTER XVIII

WASHINGTON'S WILL

PROBABLY there is no better index to a man's life and the secret of his heart than his "last will and testament," when he calmly faces death and the realities of the hereafter. In the final accounting of his stewardship, his true character is manifested.

Four *items* in his will are of special interest at this time, as they indicate his benevolent character:

(1) GIVES BIBLE

"To the reverend, now Bryan Lord Fairfax, I give a Bible, in three large folio volumes, with notes presented to me by the Rt. Rev. *Thomas Wilson*, bishop of Sodor and Man."[295]

(2) PROVIDES FOR RELEASE OF DEBT AND SLAVES

"*Item.*—The balance due me from the estate of *Bartholomew Dandridge*, deceased (my wife's brother), and which amounted, on the first day of October, 1795, to 425 l. [pounds] (as will appear by an account rendered by his deceased son, *John Dandridge*, who was the acting executor of his father's will), I release and acquit from the payment thereof. And the

237

negroes (then 33 in number) formerly belonging to
the said estate, who were taken in execution, sold,
and purchased in on my account, in the year ——,
and ever since have remained in the possession and to
the use of *Mary*, widow of the said Barth. Dandridge, with their increase, it is my will and desire,
shall continue and be in her possession, without paying any hire, or making compensation for the same,
for the time past or to come, during her natural life;
at the expiration of which, I direct, that all of them
who are 40 years old and upwards, shall receive their
freedom; all under that age and above 16, shall serve
seven years, and no longer; and all under 16 years,
shall serve until they are 25 years of age, and then
be free.   And to avoid disputes respecting the ages
of any of these negroes, they are to be taken into the
court of the county in which they reside, and the
judgment thereof, in this relation, shall be final and
record made thereof, which may be adduced as evidence at any time thereafter, if disputes should arise
concerning the same.   And I further direct, that the
heirs of the said *Barth. Dandridge* shall equally
share the benefits arising from the services of the said
negroes, according to the tenor of this devise, upon
the decease of their mother."[296]

(3) PROVIDES FOR FREEDOM OF SLAVES

"*Item.*—Upon the decease of my wife, it is my will
and desire, that all the slaves which I hold in *my own
right*, shall receive their freedom.   To emancipate
them during her life, would, though earnestly wished

by me, be attended with such insuperable difficulties, on account of their intermixture by marriages with
the dower negroes, as to excite the most painful sen-
sations, if not disagreeable consequences to the latter,
while both descriptions are in the occupancy of the
same proprietor; it not being in my power, under
the tenure by which the dower negroes are held, to
manumit them. And whereas, among those who
will receive freedom according to this devise, there
may be some who, from old age or bodily infirmities,
and others who, on account of their infancy, will be
unable to support themselves, it is my will and desire,
that all who come under the first and second description, shall be comfortably clothed and fed by my
heirs while they live; and that such of the latter description as have no parents living, or, if living, are
unable or unwilling to provide for them, shall be
bound by the court until they shall arrive at the age
of 25 years; and in cases where no record can be produced, whereby their ages can be ascertained, the
judgment of the court, upon its own view of the subject, shall be adequate and final. The negroes thus
bound, are, (by their masters or mistresses,) to be
taught to read and write, and be brought up to some
useful occupation, agreeably to the laws of the commonwealth of Virgina, providing for the support of
orphan and other poor children. And I do hereby
expressly forbid the sale or transportation out of the
said commonwealth of any slave I may die possessed
of, under any pretence whatsoever. And I do more-
over most pointedly and most solemnly enjoin it upon

my executors hereafter named, or the survivors of them, to see that *this* clause respecting slaves, and every part thereof, be religiously fulfilled at the epoch at which it is directed to take place, without evasion, neglect, or delay, after the crops which may then be on the ground are harvested, particularly as it respects the aged and infirm; seeing that a regular and permanent fund be established for their support as long as they are subjects requiring it, not trusting to the uncertain provisions made by individuals.—And, to my mulatto man, *William* (calling himself William Lee) I give immediate freedom, or if he should prefer it, (on account of the accidents which have befallen him, and which have rendered him incapable of walking, or of any active employment,) to remain in the situation he now is, it shall be optional in him to do so; in either case, however, I allow him an annuity of 30 dollars during his natural life, which shall be independent of the victuals and clothes he has been accustomed to receive, if he chooses the latter alternative; but in full with his freedom, if he prefers the first; and this I give him as a testimony of my sense of his attachment to me, and for his faithful services during the revolutionary war."[297]

(4) Bequest to Academy at Alexandria

"*Item.*—To the trustees, governors, or by whatsoever other name they may be designated, of the academy in the town of Alexandria, I give and bequeath, in trust, four thousand dollars, or in other words, twenty of the shares which I hold in the bank of Alexandria, toward the support of a free school, established at, and annexed to the said academy, for the purpose of educating orphan children, or the children of such other poor and indigent persons as are unable to accomplish it with their own means, and who, in the judgment of the trustees of the said seminary, are best entitled to the benefit of this donation. The aforesaid twenty shares I give and bequeath in perpetuity, the dividends only of which are to be drawn for, and applied by the said trustees, for the time being, for the uses above mentioned, the stock to remain entire and untouched, unless indications of failure of the said bank should be so apparent, or a discontinuance thereof shall render a removal of this fund necessary. In either of these cases, the amount of the stock here devised is to be vested in some other bank or public institution, whereby the interest may with regularity and certainty be drawn and applied as above. And, to prevent misconception, my meaning is, and is hereby declared to be, that these twenty shares are in lieu of, and not in addition to, the 1000 pounds given by a missive letter some years ago, in consequence whereof an annuity of 50 pounds has since been paid towards the support of this institution."[298]

CHAPTER XIX
HIS RELIGIOUS HABITS

No attempt has been made to group the facts in Washington's religious life so as to emphasize any particular phase. We have followed him step by step, and year by year, letting him speak and act for himself. The careful student cannot fail to be impressed with the continuity and steady development of his religious character, and the fullness of its expression throughout his whole life. The evidence is all in. The reader is the judge. Some corroborative testimony and the opinions of others may help to form a right conclusion.

A LETTER BY MISS NELLY CUSTIS

I shall here insert a letter on this subject, written to the historian Jared Sparks, by Nelly Custis, who lived twenty years in Washington's family, and who was his adopted daughter, and the granddaughter of Mrs. Washington. The testimony it affords, and the hints it contains respecting the domestic habits of Washington, are interesting and valuable.

HIS RELIGIOUS HABITS

Sir:

I received your favor of the 20th instant last evening, and hasten to give you the information which you desire.

Truro Parish is the one in which Mount Vernon, Pohick Church, and Woodlawn are situated. Fairfax Parish is now Alexandria. Before the Federal District was ceded to Congress Alexandria was in Fairfax County. General Washington had a pew in Pohick Church, and one in Christ Church at Alexandria. He was very instrumental in establishing Pohick Church, and I believe subscribed largely. His pew was near the pulpit. I have a perfect recollection of being there, before his election to the presidency, with him and my grandmother. It was a beautiful church, and had a large, respectable and wealthy congregation, who were regular attendants.

He attended the church at Alexandria when the weather and roads permitted a ride of ten miles. In New York and Philadelphia he never omitted attendance at church in the morning, unless detained by indisposition. The afternoon was spent in his own room at home; the evening with his family, and without company. Sometimes an old and intimate friend called to see us for an hour or two; but visiting and visitors were prohibited for that day. No one in church attended to the service with more reverential respect. My grandmother, who was eminently pious, never deviated from her early habits. She always knelt. The General, as was then the custom,

243

stood during the devotional parts of the service. On communion Sundays he left the church with me, after the blessing, and returned home, and we sent the carriage back for my grandmother.

It was his custom to retire to his library at nine or ten o'clock, where he remained an hour before he went to his chamber. He always rose before the sun, and remained in his library until called for breakfast. I never *witnessed* his private devotions. I never *inquired* about them. I should have thought it the greatest heresy to doubt his firm belief in Christianity. His life, his writings, prove that he was a Christian. He was not one of those who act or pray, "that they may be seen of men." He communed with his God in secret.

My mother resided two years at Mount Vernon, after her marriage with John Parke Custis, the only son of Mrs. Washington. I have heard her say that General Washington always received the sacrament with my grandmother before the Revolution. When my aunt, Miss Custis, died suddenly at Mount Vernon, before they could realize the event, he knelt by her and prayed most fervently, most affectingly, for her recovery. Of this I was assured by Judge Washington's mother, and other witnesses.

He was a silent, thoughtful man. He spoke little generally; never of himself. I never heard him relate a single act of his life during the war. I have often seen him perfectly abstracted, his lips moving, but no sound was perceptible. I have sometimes made him laugh most heartily from sympathy with my joyous and extravagant spirits. I was, probably, one of the last persons on earth to whom he would have addressed serious conversation, particularly when he knew that I had the most perfect model of female excellence ever with me as my monitress, who acted the part of a tender and devoted parent, loving me as only a mother can love, and never extenuating or approving in me what she disapproved in others. She never omitted her private devotions, or her public duties; and she and her husband were so perfectly united and happy that he must have been a Christian. She had no doubts, no fears for him. After forty years of devoted affection and uninterrupted happiness, she resigned him without a murmur into the arms of his Saviour and his God, with the assured hope of eternal felicity. Is it necessary that any one should certify, "General Washington avowed himself to *me* a believer in Christianity"? As well may we question his patriotism, his heroic, disinterested devotion to his country. His mottoes were, "*Deeds, Not Words*"; and, "*For God and My Country.*"

With sentiments of esteem,
I am, etc.[299]

Testimony of Mr. Robert Lewis

Mr. Jared Sparks, the historian, adds the following:

"It seems proper to subjoin to this letter what was told to me by Mr. Robert Lewis, at Fredericksburg, in the year 1827. Being a nephew of Washington, and his private secretary during the first part of his presidency, Mr. Lewis lived with him on terms of intimacy, and had the best opportunity for observing his habits. Mr. Lewis said he had accidentally witnessed his private devotions in his library both morning and evening; that on those occasions he had seen him in a kneeling posture with a Bible open before him, and that he believed such to have been his daily practice. Mr. Lewis is since dead, but he was a gentleman esteemed for his private worth and respectability. I relate the anecdote as he told it to me, understanding at the time that he was willing it should be made public on his authority. He added, that it was the President's custom to go to his library in the morning at four o'clock, and that, after his devotions, he usually spent his time till breakfast in writing letters."[300]

A LETTER BY BISHOP WHITE

The following letter from the venerable Bishop White was written to the Rev. B. C. C. Parker, then rector of Trinity Church in Lenox, Massachusetts:

PHILADELPHIA, 28 November, 1832.
DEAR SIR:

I have received your letter of the 20th instant,

and will furnish you with what information I possess on the subject of it.

[The first paragraph of this letter is quoted on page 238.]

Although I was often in company with this great man, and had the honor of dining often at his table, I never heard anything from him which could manifest his opinions on the subject of religion. I knew no man who so carefully guarded against the discoursing of himself, or of his acts, or of any thing that pertained to him; and it has occasionally occurred to me when in his company that, if a stranger to his person were present, he would never have known from anything said by the President that he was conscious of having distinguished himself in the eye of the world. His ordinary behavior, although exceptionally courteous, was not such as to encourage obtrusion on what he had on his mind.

Within a few days of his leaving the Presidential chair our vestry waited on him with an address, prepared and delivered by me. In his answer he was pleased to express himself gratified by what he had heard from our pulpit; but there was nothing that committed him relatively to religious theory. Within a day or two of the above there was another address by many ministers of different persuasions, being prepared by Doctor Green and delivered by me. It has been a subject of opposite statements, owing to a passage in the posthumous works of Mr. Jefferson. He says (giving Doctor Rush for his author, who is said to have it from Doctor Green), that the said address was intended to elicit the opinion of the President on the subject of the Christian religion. Doctor Green has denied this in his periodical work called "*The Christian Advocate*," and his statement is correct. Doctor Rush may have misunderstood Doctor Green, or the former may have been misunderstood by Mr. Jefferson; or the whole may have originated with some individual of the assembled ministers, who mistook his own conceptions for the sense of the body. The said two documents are in the Philadelphia newspapers of the time.

On a thanksgiving day, appointed by the President for the suppression of the Western insurrection, I preached in his presence. The subject was the Connection between Religion and Civil Happiness. It was misrepresented in one of our newspapers. This induced the publishing of the sermon, with a dedication to the President, pointedly pleading his proclamation in favor of the connection affirmed. It did not appear that he disallowed the use made of his name. Although, in my estimation, entire separation between Christianity and civil government would be a relinquishment of religion in the abstract; yet, that this was the sentiment of the President, which may have been, I have no light positively to infer.

There do not occur to me any other particulars meeting your inquiry, confined to my knowledge. Accordingly I conclude with writing myself, very respectfully, your humble servant,

WILLIAM WHITE.[301]

CLAIMED TO BE A CHURCHMAN

When Washington was passing through Litchfield, Connecticut, during the war, there was some desecration of the church, recalling the treatment of the cathedral in old Litchfield, England, by the soldiers of Cromwell. Washington himself saw some of his soldiers throw a shower of stones at the church, and at once rebuked them. He did not put forward the merely just argument that such acts were disorderly, but he put his personal feeling into what he said: "I am a churchman, and wish not to see the church dishonored and desolated in this manner."[302]

CHAPTER XX

ESTIMATE OF HIS CHARACTER

SERMONS and orations by divines and statesmen were delivered all over the land at the death of Washington. A large volume of such was published. I have seen and read them, and the religious character of Washington was a most prominent feature in them; and for this there must have been some good cause. "That Washington was regarded throughout America, both among our military and political men, as a sincere believer in Christianity, as then received among us, and a devout man, is as clear as any fact in our history."[303]

DECLARATIONS OF HIS CONTEMPORARIES

(1) *Major-General Henry Lee*

Major-General Henry Lee, member of Congress from Virginia, who served under him during the war, and afterward in the civil department, and who was chosen by Congress to deliver his funeral oration, Thursday, December 26, 1799, at Philadelphia, in the German Lutheran Church, says in that oration: "First in war, first in peace, and first in the hearts of his countrymen, he was second to none in the humble and endearing scenes of private life. Pious, just, humane, temperate, and sincere; uniform, dignified, and commanding, his example was edifying to all around him, as were the effects of that example lasting."[304]

(2) *Jonathan Mitchell Sewall*

On Tuesday, December 31, 1799, Jonathan Mitchell Sewall delivered an oration at Portsmouth, New Hampshire, at the request of the inhabitants, in which he says:

"To crown all these moral virtues, he had the deepest sense of religion impressed on his heart—the true foundation-stone of all the moral virtues.

"This he constantly manifested on all proper occasions. He was a firm believer in the Christian religion; and, at his first entrance on his civil administration he made it known, and adhered to his purpose, that no secular business could be transacted with him on the day set apart by Christians for the worship of Deity.

"Though he was, from principle, a member of the Episcopal Church, he was candid and liberal in the highest degree, not only to all sects and denominations of Christians but to all religions, where the possessors were sincere, throughout the world.

"He constantly attended the public worship

of God on the Lord's Day, was communicant at His table, and, by his devout and solemn deportment, inspired every beholder with some portion of that awe and reverence for the Supreme Being of which he felt so large a portion.

"For my own part, I trust I shall never lose the impression made on my own mind in beholding in this house of prayer [see page 176], the venerable hero, the victorious leader of our hosts, bending in humble adoration to the God of armies, and great Captain of our salvation. Hard and unfeeling indeed must that heart be that could sustain the sight unmoved, or its owner depart unsoftened and unedified.

"Let the deist reflect on this, and remember that Washington, the saviour of his country, did not disdain to acknowledge and adore a great Saviour, whom deists and infidels affect to slight and despise."[305]

(3) *Reverend John Thornton Kirkland*

In a discourse on the death of Washington, delivered by the Rev. John Thornton Kirkland, minister of the New South Church, Boston, Massachusetts, December 29, 1799, he says: "The virtues of our departed friend were crowned with piety. He is known to have been habitually devout. To Christian institutions he gave the countenance of his example; and no one could express more fully his sense of the Providence of God, and the dependence of man."[306]

(4) *Captain Josiah Dunham*

Josiah Dunham, Captain of the 16th U. S. Regiment of the Revolution, in his funeral oration pronounced at Oxford, Massachusetts, at the request of the field officers of the brigade, stationed at that place, on the 15th of January, 1800, says of him: "A friend to our holy religion, he was ever guided by its pious doctrines. He had embraced the tenets of the Episcopal Church; yet his charity, unbounded as his immortal mind, led him equally to respect every denomination of the followers of Jesus."[307]

(5) *The Hon. David Ramsay*

The Hon. David Ramsay, M.D., of South Carolina, the historian, in his oration on the death of Washington, delivered at Charleston, South Carolina, on January 15, 1800, at the request of the inhabitants, says: "He was the friend of morality and religion; steadily attended on public worship; encouraged and strengthened the hands of the clergy. In all his public acts he made the most respectful mention of Providence, and, in a word, carried the spirit of piety with him, both in his private life and public administration. He was far from being

one of those minute philosophers who believe
that 'death is an eternal sleep;' or, of those,
who, trusting to the sufficiency of human reason,
discard the light of divine revelation."[308]

(6) *The Rev. John M. Mason, D.D.*

The Rev. Doctor John M. Mason, pastor of
the Associate Reformed Church in the city of
New York, in the funeral eulogy delivered by
appointment of a number of the clergy of New
York City, February 22, 1800, uses this language: "That invisible hand which guarded him
at first continued to guard and to guide him
through the successive stages of the Revolution.
Nor did he account it a weakness to bend the
knee in homage to its supremacy, and prayer for
its direction. This was the armor of Washington, this the salvation of his country."[309]

(7) *Jeremiah Smith*

In an oration delivered by Jeremiah Smith at
Exeter, New Hampshire, February 22, 1800, he
says:

"He had all the genuine mildness of Christianity with all its force. He was neither ostentatious, nor ashamed of his Christian profes-
sion. He pursued in this, as in every thing else,
the happy mean between the extremes of levity
and gloominess, indifference and austerity. His

religion became him. He brought it with him into office, and he did not lose it there. His first and his last official acts (as he did all the intermediate ones) contained an explicit acknowledgment of the overruling providence of the Supreme Being; and the most fervent supplication for His benediction on our government and nation.

"Without being charged with exaggeration, I may be permitted to say, that an accurate knowledge of his life, while it would confer on him the highest title to praise, would be productive of the most solid advantage to the cause of Christianity."[310]

(8) *President Timothy Dwight*

Timothy Dwight, D.D., president of Yale College, in a discourse on "The Character of Washington," February 22, 1800, says: "For my own part, I have considered his numerous and uniform public and most solemn declarations of his high veneration for religion, his exemplary and edifying attention to public worship, and his constancy in secret devotion, as proofs, sufficient to satisfy every person, willing to be satisfied. I shall only add that if he was not a Christian, he was more like one than any man of the same description whose life has been hitherto recorded."[311]

(9) *Reverend Devereux Jarratt*

In an address delivered by the Rev. Devereux
Jarratt, in Dinwiddie County, Virginia, he says:
"Washington was a professor of Christianity
and a member of the Protestant Episcopal
Church. He always acknowledged the superintendence of Divine Providence; and from his
inimitable writings we find him a warm advocate for a sound morality founded on the principles of religion, the only basis on which it can
stand. Nor did I ever meet with the most distant insinuation that his private life was not a
comment on his own admired page."[312]

Testimony of an English Sympathizer

The testimony of the Rev. Jonathan Boucher,
who, to say the least, was not prejudiced in favor
of Washington, is very interesting. He was a
minister in the Episcopal Church at Annapolis,
Maryland. During the first six months of 1775
he always preached with a pair of loaded pistols
lying on the cushion in front of him; and indeed,
with no aid from fire arms, he was well known to
be more than a match for any single member of
his congregation. He opposed the independence of the colonies, and returned to England
in 1775. He was for a time private tutor to
John Parke Custis, the son of Mrs. Washington.
His acquaintance with Washington was prior to

the Revolution, and, in his own words, he "did know Washington well." In 1776 he writes concerning him: "In his moral character he is regular, temperate, strictly just and honest (except that as a Virginian he has lately found out that there is no moral turpitude in not paying what he confesses he owes to a British creditor), and, I always thought, religious; having heretofore been pretty constant and even exemplary in his attendance on public worship in the Church of England."[313]

Such was his character, "that even in England not one reflection was ever cast, or the least disrespectful word uttered against him."[314]

TESTIMONY OF OTHERS

(1) *President Madison*

President Madison says, "Washington was constant in the observance of worship, according to the received forms of the Episcopal Church."[315]

(2) *Robert C. Winthrop*

Robert C. Winthrop, acknowledging the receipt of the Rev. Philip Slaughter's oration on Washington, says, "It confirms all my opinions of the character of Washington, and leaves no loop to hang a doubt upon that Christianity was the key to that character."[316]

(3) *Bushrod Washington*

Washington bequeathed Mount Vernon, four thousand acres, including the Mansion House to his nephew, Bushrod Washington, who afterwards became a judge of the Supreme Court of the United States. In 1826 the latter was elected a vice-president of the American Sunday School Union. In replying to an address he said, "Upon the well-intended efforts I have made to secure the due observance of the Sabbath day, upon a spot, where, I am persuaded, it was never violated during the life and with the permission of its venerable owner."[317]

Tradition of the New York Indians

The New York Indians hold this tradition of Washington: "Alone, of all white men, he has been admitted to the Indian Heaven, because of his justice to the Red Men. He lives in a great palace, built like a fort. All the Indians, as they go to Heaven, pass by, and he himself is in his uniform, a sword at his side, walking to and fro. They bow reverently with great humility. He returns the salute, but says nothing." Such is the reward of his justice to the Red Man.[318]

Abraham and Washington

The Rev. Israel Evans was a chaplain in the United States army through nearly the entire

Revolutionary service. He was a native of New Jersey, a man of education, and capable of appreciating such a character as that of Washington. The opportunities he enjoyed for social intercourse with him, as well as with other patriots of the Revolution, were very frequent and favorable, and his reverence for Washington was very great.

"It is related of Mr. Evans that during his last sickness, thirty years or more after the Revolution, his successor in the ministry, in the New England village where he had been settled, was called in by the family to pray with him, in the evident near approach of the dying hour. Mr. Evans had lain some considerable time in a stupor, apparently unconscious of anything around him, and his brother clergyman was proceeding in a fervent prayer to God, that, as his servant was evidently about departing this mortal life, his spirit might be conveyed by angels to Abraham's bosom. Just at this point, the dying man for the first time and for the moment revived, so far as to utter, in an interval of his delirium, '*and Washington's, too*'—and then sunk again into apparent unconsciousness. As if it was not enough to 'have *Abraham* to his father,' and on whose bosom to repose, but he must have *Washington*, too, on whom to lean. A signal manifestation of 'the ruling passion strong in death'— and of the lasting hold which that great man had on the mind and heart of one of his early and devoted friends."[319]

Judgment of Historians

(1) *Mason L. Weems*

"The noblest, the most efficient element of his character was that he was an humble, earnest Christian."[320]

(2) *Aaron Bancroft*

"In principle and practice he was a *Christian.*"[321]

(3) *Cyrus R. Edmonds*

"The elements of his greatness are chiefly to be discovered in the moral features of his character."[322]

(4) *John Marshall*

Chief Justice John Marshall, who had been the personal friend and frequent associate of Washington, says in his biography, "Without making ostentatious professions of religion, he was a sincere believer in the Christian faith, and a truly devout man."[323]

(5) *George Bancroft*

"Belief in God and trust in His overruling power, formed the essence of his character. . . . His whole being was one continued act of faith in the eternal, intelligent and moral order of the universe."[324]

(6) *Jared Sparks*

"A Christian in faith and practice, he was habitually devout. His reverence for religion is seen in his example, his public communications, and his private writings. He uniformly ascribed his successes to the beneficent agency of the Supreme Being. Charitable and humane, he was liberal to the poor and kind to those in distress. As a husband, son, and brother, he was tender and affectionate."[325]

"If a man spoke, wrote, and acted as a Christian through a long life, who gave numerous proofs of his believing himself to be such, and who was never known to say, write or do a thing contrary to his professions, if such a man is not to be ranked among the believers of Christianity, it would be impossible to establish the point by any train of reasoning. . . .

"After a long and minute examination of the writings of Washington, public and private, in print and in manuscript, I can affirm that I have never seen a single hint or expression from which it could be inferred that he had any doubt of the Christian revelation, or that he thought with indifference or unconcern of that subject. On the contrary, whenever he approaches it, and, indeed, whenever he alludes in any manner to religion, it is done with seriousness and reverence."[326]

261

CHAPTER XXI

THE VERDICT

(1) DAVID RAMSAY

DOCTOR DAVID RAMSAY was a celebrated physician of Charleston, South Carolina. He was a delegate to the Continental Congress in 1782–86. In his biography of Washington, one of the best ever published, he says: "There are few men of any kind, and still fewer of those the world calls great, who have not some of their virtues eclipsed by corresponding vices. But this was not the case with General Washington. He had religion without austerity, dignity without pride, modesty without diffidence, courage without rashness, politeness without affectation, affability without familiarity. His private character, as well as his public one, will bear the strictest scrutiny. He was punctual in all his engagements; upright and honest in his dealings; temperate in his enjoyments; liberal and hospitable to an eminent degree; a lover of order; systematical and methodical in his arrangements. He was a friend of morality and religion; steadily attended on public worship; encouraged and strengthened the hands of the

262

clergy. In all his public acts he made the most respectful mention of Providence; and, in a word, carried the spirit of piety with him both in his private life and public administration."[327]

(2) JAMES K. PAULDING

"It is impossible to read the speeches and letters of Washington and follow his whole course of life, without receiving the conviction of his steady, rational, and exalted piety. Everywhere he places his chief reliance, in the difficult, almost hopeless circumstances in which he was so often involved, on the justice of that great Being who holds the fate of men and of nations in the hollow of His hand. His hopes for his country are always founded on the righteousness of its cause, and the blessing of Heaven. His was the belief of reason and revelation; and that belief was illustrated and exemplified in all his actions. No parade accompanied its exercises, no declamation its exhibition; for it was his opinion that a man who is always boasting of his religion, is like one who continually proclaims his honesty—he would trust neither one nor the other. He was not accustomed to argue points of faith, but on one occasion, in reply to a gentleman who expressed doubts on the subject, thus gave his sentiments:

" 'It is impossible to account for the creation

of the universe without the agency of a Supreme Being.

" 'It is impossible to govern the universe without the aid of a Supreme Being.

" 'It is impossible to reason without arriving at a Supreme Being. Religion is as necessary to reason as reason is to religion. The one cannot exist without the other. A reasoning being would lose his reason in attempting to account for the great phenomena of nature, had he not a Supreme Being to refer to; and well has it been said, that if there had been no God, mankind would have been obliged to imagine one.' "[328]

"On this basis of piety was erected the superstructure of his virtues. He perceived the harmonious affinity subsisting between the duties we owe to Heaven and those we are called upon to sustain on earth, and made his faith the foundation of his moral obligations. He cherished the homely but invaluable maxim that 'honesty is the best policy,' and held that the temporal as well as eternal happiness of mankind could never be separated from the performance of their duties to Heaven and their fellow creatures. He believed it to be an inflexible law that, sooner or later, a departure from the strict obligations of truth and justice would bring with it the loss of confidence of mankind, and thus deprive us of our best support for prosperity in this world, as well as our best hope of happiness in that to come. In short, he believed and practiced on the high principle, that the invariable consequence of the performance of a duty was an increase of happiness. What others call good fortune, he ascribed to a great and universal law, establishing an indissoluble connection between actions and their consequences, and making every man responsible to himself for his good or ill success in this world. Under that superintending Providence which shapes the ends of men, his sentiments and actions show that he believed, that, as a general rule, every rational being was the architect of his own happiness."[329]

(3) SIR GEORGE OTTO TREVELYAN

The following, by this noted English writer, is very interesting:

"A better churchman—or, at all events, a better man who ranked himself as a churchman —than George Washington it would have been hard indeed to discover. When at home on the bank of the Potomac, he had always gone of a Sunday morning to what would have been called a distant church by any one except a Virginia equestrian; and he spent Sunday afternoons, alone and unapproachable, in his library. In war he found time for daily prayer and meditation (as, by no wish of his, the absence of privacy, which is a feature in camp life, revealed to those who were immediately about him); he attended public worhsip himself; and by every available means he encouraged the practice of religion in his soldiers, to whom he habitually stood in a kind of fatherly relation. There are many pages in his Orderly Books which indicate a determination that the multitude of young fellows who were intrusted to his charge should have all possible facilities for being as well-behaved as in their native villages.

"The troops were excused fatigue duty in order that they might not miss church. If public worship was interrupted on a Sunday by the call to arms, a service was held on a convenient day in the ensuing week. The chaplains were exhorted to urge the soldiers that they ought to live and act like Christian men in times of distress and danger; and after every great victory, and more particularly at the final proclamation of Peace, the Commander-in-chief earnestly recommended that the army should universally attend the rendering of thanks to Almighty God 'with seriousness of deportment and gratitude of heart.' "[330]

"Washington loved his own church the best, and had no mind to leave it; but he was not hostile to any faith which was sincerely held, and which exerted a restraining and correcting influence upon human conduct. 'I am disposed,' he once told Lafayette, 'to indulge the professors of Christianity with that road to Heaven which to them shall seem the most direct, plainest, easiest, and least liable to exception.' His feeling on this matter was accurately expressed in the instructions which he wrote out for Benedict Arnold, when that officer led an armed force of fierce and stern New England Protestants against the Roman Catholic settlements in Canada. The whole paper was a lesson in the statesmanship which is founded on respect and consideration for others, and still remains well worth reading. In after years, as President of the United States, Washington enjoyed frequent opportunities for impressing his own sentiments and policy, in all that related to religion, upon the attention of his compatriots. The churches of America were never tired of framing and presenting addresses which assured him of their confidence, veneration, and sympathy; and he as invariably replied by congratulating them that in their country worship was free, and that men of every creed were eligible to every post of honor and authority."[331]

(4) HENRY CABOT LODGE

"He had the same confidence in the judgment of posterity that he had in the future beyond the grave. He regarded death with entire calmness, and even indifference, not only when it came to him, but when in previous years it had threatened him. He loved life and tasted of it deeply, but the courage which never forsook him made him ready to face the inevitable at any moment with an unruffled spirit. In this he was helped by his religious faith, which was as simple as it was profound. He had been brought up in the Protestant Episcopal Church, and to that church he always adhered, for its splendid liturgy and stately forms appealed to him and satisfied him. He loved it too as the church of his home and his childhood. Yet he was as far as possible from being sectarian, and there is not a word of his which shows anything but the most entire liberality and toleration. He made no parade of his religion, for in this, as in other things, he was perfectly simple and sincere. He was tortured by no doubts or questionings, but believed always in an overruling Providence and in a merciful God, to whom he knelt and prayed in the day of darkness or in the hour of triumph with a supreme and childlike confidence."[332]

What Made Him Great

"When the children of the years to come, hearing his great name re-echoed from every lip, shall say to their fathers, 'What was it that raised Washington to such height of glory?' let them be told that it was HIS GREAT TALENTS, CONSTANTLY GUIDED AND GUARDED BY RELIGION.''[333]

"The purest and noblest character of modern time—possibly of all time."—*Duke of Wellington.*

SOURCES OF INFORMATION

FOLLOWING are the titles of the seventy-five volumes from which the material in this book has been drawn. The first word is the surname of the author, or a part of the title of the book, magazine, etc. It is the "key-word" used in "Where Found" on p. 276. The date given is the date of publication, although it is not in every case the date of the first edition.

APPLETON: Appleton's Cyclopædia of American Biography, Vol. VI, 1889.

BAKER: Character Portraits of Washington, by William S. Baker, 1887.
Early Sketches of George Washington, by William S. Baker, 1894.
Itinerary of General Washington, 1775-1783, by William S. Baker, 1892.
Washington after the Revolution, 1784-1799, by William S. Baker, 1897.

BALDWIN: An American Book of Golden Deeds, by James Baldwin, 1907.

BANCROFT: Life of George Washington, by Aaron Bancroft, 1807.

BANCROFT: History of the United States, by George Bancroft, Vol VII, 1888.

BARNES: Christian Keepsake, by Rev. Albert Barnes, D.D., 1840.

SOURCES OF INFORMATION

BURK: Washington's Prayers, by W. Herbert Burk, 1907. Dr. Burk very graciously gave permission to reprint these "Prayers" in this book.

BUTLER: Washington at Valley Forge, by J. M. Butler, 1858.

CHRONICLE: London Chronicle, September 21–23, 1779.

CLARK: Colonial Churches, by W. M. Clark, 1907.

CONWAY: George Washington's Rules of Civility, by Moncure D. Conway, 1890.

CUSTIS: Recollections and Private Memoirs of Washington, by George Washington Parke Custis, Edited by Benson J. Lossing, 1860.

Much of the material in this book appeared in different publications as early as 1827.

George Washington Parke Custis was the grandson of Mrs. Washington. He was born in 1781. Six months later his father died. His father was the son of Mrs. Washington by a former marriage. Upon the death of his father he was adopted by General Washington, and lived with him at Mount Vernon as his own son. Mr. Custis died in 1857 in the seventy-seventh year of his age. He was, therefore, in his nineteenth year when Washington died.

DIARY: The Diary of George Washington, from 1789 to 1791, Edited by Benson J. Lossing, 1860.

DUDLEY: The Cambridge of 1776, with the Diary of Dorothy Dudley, 1876.

EDMONDS: Life and Times of General Washington, by Cyrus R. Edmonds (England), 2 Vols., 1835.

EULOGIES AND ORATIONS: Eulogies and Orations on the Life and Death of General George Washington, 1800.

FORD: The True George Washington, by Paul Leicester Ford, 1903.

GREEN: The Life of Ashabel Green, by Himself, 1849.

HALE: Contemplations: Moral and Divine, by Sir Matthew Hale, Knight; late Chief Justice of the King's Bench. Printed in London, 1695.

HARLAND: The Story of Mary Washington, by Marion Harland, 1892.

HARPER: Harper's Magazine, 1859.

HOSACK: Memoir of DeWitt Clinton, by David Hosack, M. D., 1829.

HOUGH: Memorials of the Death of Washington, by Franklin B. Hough, 1865.

IRVING: Life of George Washington, by Washington Irving, 5 Vols., 1857.

JOHNSTON: George Washington, Day by Day, by Elizabeth Bryant Johnston, 1894.

KIRKLAND: Memoirs of Washington, by Mrs. C. M. Kirkland, 1857.

SOURCES OF INFORMATION

LITTELL: George Washington: Christian, by Rev. John Stockton Littell, D.D., 1913.

LODGE: George Washington, by Henry Cabot Lodge, 2 Vols., 1898.

LONG ISLAND: Memoirs of the Long Island Historical Society, Vol. IV, 1889.

LOSSING: Mary and Martha Washington, by Benson J. Lossing, 1886.

The Pictorial Field-Book of the Revolution, by Benson J. Lossing, 2 Vols., 1860.

MARSHALL: The Life of George Washington, by John Marshall, Abridged Edition, 2 Vols., 1832. (First edition in 1804-7, 5 Vols.)

He was chosen by the Washington Family to write the biography of George Washington.

MEADE: Old Churches, Ministers and Families of Virginia, by Bishop Meade, 2 Vols., 1872. The author was Bishop of Virginia for 33 years (1829–1862).

M'GUIRE: The Religious Opinions and Character of Washington, by Rev. E. C. M'Guire, 1836.

Mr. M'Guire married the daughter of Mr. Robert Lewis, the nephew and private secretary of Washington, and thus he had exceptional sources of information.

MOORE: Libels on George Washington, by George H. Moore, 1889.

NORTON: Life of General Washington, by John N. Norton, 1870.

PAULDING: A life of Washington, by James K. Paulding, 2 Vols., 1836.

POST: Pennsylvania Evening Post, Philadelphia, April 9, 1776.

POTTER: Washington in His Library and Life, by President Eliphalet Nott Potter, 1895.

PRESBYTERIAN: The Presbyterian Magazine, Edited by C. Van Rensselaer, Philadelphia, Pa., February, 1851.

PRYOR: The Mother of George Washington and Her Times, by Mrs. Roger A. Pryor, 1903.

RAMSAY: Life of George Washington, by David Ramsay, M.D., 1807.

RUSH: Washington in Domestic Life, by Richard Rush, 1857.

SHERMAN: Historic Morristown, New Jersey, by Andrew M. Sherman, 1905.

SMITH: Orderly Book of the Siege of Yorktown, Edited by Horace W. Smith, 1865.

SPARKS: The writings of George Washington, by Jared Sparks, 12 Vols., 1834-7.

THACHER: Military Journal during the American Revolutionary War, from 1775 to 1783, by James Thacher, M.D., 1823.

TONER: Washington's Barbadoes Journal, 1751-2, Edited by J. M. Toner, M.D., 1892.

TREVELYAN: The American Revolution, by the Right Hon. Sir George Trevelyan, Bart., 1908.

SOURCES OF INFORMATION

TRIBUNE: New York Tribune, May 26, 1902.

VERNON: General Washington, the American Soldier and Christian, by Merle Vernon.

WALTER: Memorials of Washington and Mary, His Mother, and Martha, His Wife, by James Walter, 1887.

WEEMS: The Life of General Washington, by the Rev. Mason L. Weems, 1808.

Two editions were published before Washington's death. These were brief biographical sketches only. The third edition, in 1800, was dedicated to Mrs. Washington. The fourth edition was in 1804. The cherry tree, cabbage seed, and other stories, which made the book famous, first appeared in the fifth edition, in 1806.

WHITING: Revolutionary Orders of General Washington, selected from MSS. of John Whiting, Edited by Henry Whiting, 1844.

Colonel John Whiting fought through all the Revolutionary War.

WYLIE: Washington, A Christian, by the Rev. Theodore Wm. John Wylie, 1862.

WHERE FOUND

THE following is a complete list of references to books, magazines, and papers, with volume and page, from which the material used in this book has been taken, together with explanatory notes.

The numbers correspond to the index numbers throughout the book.

A "key-word" is used, by means of which the full title of the book or magazine from which the material is taken, may readily be found by reference to the same word under "Sources of Information" on page 270.

Illustration: On page 69 is the index number "77" Turning to "Where Found" we find opposite 77, "Norton, p. 145." Under "Sources of Information," opposite the word "Norton," is "Life of General Washington, by John N. Norton, 1870." This is the book, published in 1870, from which the extract is taken, and it is found on page 145.

[1] Littell, p. 5.
[2] M'Guire, p. 31.
[3] Walter, p. 123.
[4] M'Guire, p. 40.
[5] Hale.
[6] Norton, p. 34.
[7] Lossing, p. 27.
[8] Irving, Vol. I, p. 49.

WHERE FOUND

[9] Conway, p. 49; [10] pp. 178, 180.

[11] Burk, p. 12.

[12] Littell, p. 7.

[13] M'Guire, p. 47.

[14] Toner, p. 49.

[15] Burk, p. 13. Experts in Washington City, Philadelphia and New York are satisfied that it is Washington's handwriting without a doubt.

[16] Burk, pp. 87–95.

[17] Harland, p. 87.

[18] Norton, p. 34.

[19] Sparks, Vol. II, p. 54.

[20] M'Guire, p. 136.

[21] Irving, Vol. I, p. 163.

[22] Sparks, Vol. II, p. 43.

[23] M'Guire, p. 137.

[24] Harland, p. 91. In writing to his mother, Washington always addressed her, "Madam." It is a term of dignity and endearment, customary at that time.

[25] M'Guire, p. 137.

[26] Sparks, Vol. II, p. 89.

[27] Custis, p. 303. This narrative was told Mr. Custis by Dr. Craik. It was first published in 1828.

[28] Sparks, Vol. II, p. 132; [29] p. 141; [30] p. 149.

[31] Sparks, Vol. II, p. 167. Extract from "Orderly Book," written two days after he reached Fort Cumberland.

[32] M'Guire, p. 70.

[33] Sparks, Vol. II, p. 188; [34] p. 200; [35] p. 200; [36] p. 201; [37] p. 203; [38] p. 278.

[39] Weems, p. 182.

[40] Lossing: Mary and Martha, p. 99.

[41] Kirkland, pp. 198, 199.

[42] Clark, p. 126; [43] p. 126.

[44] Lossing: Field-Book, Vol. II, p. 215.

[45] Clark, p. 121; [46] p. 126; [47] p. 113; [48] p. 130; [49] p. 118.

[50] Norton, p. 112.

[51] Clark, p. 126.

[52] Norton, p. 112; [53] p. 112.

[54] Irving, Vol. I, p. 365.

[55] M'Guire, p. 141; [56] p. 142.

[57] Tribune, p. 7, by the Rev. Randolph H. M'Kim, D.D., Rector of the Church of the Epiphany, Washington, D. C.

[58] M'Guire, p. 411.

[59] Presbyterian, p. 70.

[60] Baker: After the Revolution, p. 40 (from Washington's Diary).

[61] Norton, p. 117.

[62] Known simply as the Episcopal Church until 1813; since then as Christ Church.—Clark, p. 137.

[63] Clark, p. 135; [64] p. 118; [65] p. 136.

[66] Norton, p. 123; Custis, p. 21.

[67] Ford, p. 29.

[68] M'Guire, p. 142.

[69] Lodge, Vol. I, p. 123.

[70] Clark, p. 136.

[71] Butler, pp. 48, 49.

[72] Irving, Vol. I, p. 461.

[73] M'Guire, p. 143.

[74] Appleton, Vol. VI, p. 383.

[75] Weems, p. 182.

[76] Sparks, Vol. III, p. 2.

[77] Norton, p. 145.

[78] Sparks, Vol. III, p. 491; [79] p. 491.

[80] Johnston, p. 107 (from "Orderly Book").

[81] Sparks, Vol. III, p. 80; [82] p. 86; [83] p. 91; [84] p. 92.

[85] Johnston, p. 146.

[86] Sparks, Vol. III, p. 171.   Mrs. Washington was on her way to Cambridge to visit General Washington.

[87] M'Guire, p. 190.

[88] Paulding, Vol. II, pp. 226, 227.

[89] Baker: Itinerary, Vol. I, p. 22.

[90] Dudley, p. 48; [91] p. 49.

[92] Sparks, Vol. III, p. 240.

[93] Sparks, Vol. III, p. 296 (from "Orderly Book").

[94] Dudley, p. 59.

[95] Sparks, Vol. IX, p. 337.

[96] Johnston, p. 41.

[97] Thacher, p. 51.

[98] Post, April 9, 1776.

[99] Sparks, Vol. III, p. 341.

[100] Meade, Vol. II, p. 251.

[101] Trevelyan, Vol. III, p. 304.

[102] Sparks, Vol. III, p. 392; [103] p. 404; [104] p. 449; [105] p. 456.

[106] Sparks, Vol. IV, p. 26.

[107] Potter, p. 124.

[108] Sherman, p. 238; [109] p. 239.

[110] Hosack, p. 183.

[111] Harper, Vol. XVIII, p. 293.

[112] Sherman, p. 237.

[113], [114], [115] M'Guire, pp. 411–414.

[116] Presbyterian, Vol. I, p. 71.

[117] Presbyterian, Vol. I, p. 569.

[118] Tribune, p. 7.

[119] Presbyterian, p. 570, Rev. O. L. Kirtland's letter.

[120] Probably the Mrs. Ford in whose house Washington had his headquarters the second winter that the army encamped at Morristown, 1780–81.

[121] Presbyterian, p. 569, Rev. O. L. Kirtland's letter.

[122] Sparks, Vol. XII, p. 409.

[123] Trevelyan, Vol. III, p. 309.

[124] Sparks, Vol. IV, p. 436; [125] p. 482.

[126] M'Guire, p. 114.

[127] Sparks, Vol. V, p. 88; [128] p. 103; [129] p. 105; [130] p. 120; [131] p. 524.

[132] Weems, p. 104.

[133] Lossing: Field-Book, Vol. II, p. 130.

[134] M'Guire, p. 158.

[135] Wylie, pp. 28, 29.

[136] M'Guire, p. 159.

[137] Barnes, p. 265.

[138] Baldwin, pp. 102–107.

[139] Sparks, Vol. V, 276.

[140] Whiting, p. 58; [141] p. 74; [142] p. 77.

[143] Lossing: Field-Book, Vol. II, p. 140.

[144] Sparks, Vol. V, p. 388.

[145] Norton, p. 253.

[146] Moore, p. 6 (p. 5).

[147] Custis, p. 413. General Scott was governor of Kentucky after the war.

[148] Sparks, Vol. V, p. 432.

[149] Sparks, Vol. VI, p. 36.

[150] Baker: Early Sketches, p. 77.

[151] Chronicle, Vol. XLVI, p. 228.

[152] M'Guire, pp. 162–167.

In the summer of 1779 Washington had his Head-Quarters on the Hudson River. That he was in the habit of traveling alone sometimes during the war is well known. The circumstances mentioned above are said to have occurred in the month of June,—the year it would seem not remembered. It appears from one of his letters that he was absent from camp for a day or two, about that time in 1779. In a letter dated New Windsor, July 9th, he says, "I did not receive intelligence of this till the *afternoon* of the 7th inst., having been absent from head-quarters from the *morning* of the preceding day, on a visit to our outposts below, and those lately established by the enemy."—M'Guire, p. 165.

[153] M'Guire, pp. 160, 161.

[154] Kirkland, p. 478.

[155] Meade, Vol. II, p. 492.

[156] Kirkland, p. 479.

[157] Custis, p. 493.

[158] M'Guire, p. 146.

[159] Bancroft (Aaron), 1808, p. 538.

[160] Thacher, p. 246.

[161] Sparks, Vol. VII, p. 449; [162] p. 462.

[163] Baker: Itinerary, p. 220 (from Diary of (Gov.) Jonathan Trumbull).

[164] Smith, p. 47.

[165] Custis, p. 38.

[166] Sparks, Vol. VIII, p. 207.

[167] Whiting, pp. 205, 206.

[168] Sparks, Vol. VIII, p. 234.

[169] Baker: After the Revolution, p. 288 (from "Orderly Book").

[170] Johnston, p. 44.

[171] Custis, p. 290.

[172] Sparks, Vol. VIII, p. 567; [173] pp. 440, 441, 452.

[174] Sparks, Vol. VIII, p. 475.

[175] M'Guire, p. 125.

[176] Johnston, p. 160.

[177] Sparks, Vol. VIII, pp. 492, 496.

[178] Johnston, p. 182.

[179] Sparks, Vol. VIII, pp. 504, 505.

[180] Clark, p. 136.

[181] M'Guire, p. 147.

[182] Custis, p. 173.

[183] Vernon, p. 48.

[184] Norton, p. 322.

[185] Custis, p. 173.

[186] Clark, p. 130. Article by Rev. George S. Somerville, Rector of Falls Church, Virginia.

[187] Sparks, Vol. IX, p. 22.

[188] Baker: After the Revolution, p. 39, [189] p. 62; [190] p. 63; [191] p. 70.

[192] Johnston, p. 70.

WHERE FOUND

[193] Baker: After the Revolution, p. 77 (from Washington's Diary).

[194] Baker: After the Revolution, p. 80.

[195] Sparks, Vol. IX, p. 397; [196], p. 262.

[197] Baker: After the Revolution, p. 94 (from Washington's Diary).

[198] Baker: After the Revolution, p. 100 (from Washington's Diary).

[199] Baker: After the Revolution, p. 105.

[200] Sparks, Vol. IX, p. 406; [201] p. 421; [202] p. 431.

[203] Baker: After the Revolution, p. 110 (from Washington's Diary).

[204] Lossing: Field-Book, Vol. II, p. 220.

[205] Sparks, Vol. XII, p. 145.

[206] Norton, pp. 333, 334.

[207] Sparks, Vol. XII, pp. 2, 4, 5.

[208] Vernon, p. 44.

[209] Sparks, Vol. XII, p. 153; [210] p. 154.

[211] Baker: Character Portraits, p. 77 (from Biographical Sketch of General George Washington, by Jedediah Morse, D.D., December 31, 1799).

[212] Sparks, Vol. XII, p. 152; [213] p. 160; [214] pp. 162, 163.

[215] Irving, Vol. V, p. 21.

[216] M'Guire, p. 206.

[217] Sparks, Vol. XII, p. 119.

[218] Lossing: Diary, pp. 12, 18, 19, 24.

[219] Diary, p. 34.

[220] Diary, p. 42.

[221] Diary, p. 50.

[222] M'Guire, p. 175.

[223] Diary, pp. 53, 55, 58.

[224] Diary, pp. 60, 61, 62.

[225] Long Island, Vol. IV, p. 311.

[226] Diary, pp. 64, 65, 68, 71, 74, 86, 89, 91, 96, 97, 98, 104, 114.

[227] Johnston, p. 45.

[228] Diary, pp. 116, 118, 121, 128.

[229] Diary, pp. 132, 136, 137, 144, 152.

[230] M'Guire, p. 174.

[231] Johnston, p. 171. The Reverend Thomas Davis assisted at Washington's funeral.

[232] M'Guire, p. 414.

[233] Meade, Vol. II, p. 490; [234] p. 490.

[235] M'Guire, p. 153; [236] p. 153.

[237] Sparks, Vol. XII, p. 408.

[238] Kirkland, p. 486.

[239] Meade, Vol. II, p. 492; [240] p. 255; [241] p. 494.

[242] M'Guire, p. 168.

[243] Green, p. 267. The Rev. Dr. Green was pastor of the Second Presbyterian Church of Philadelphia at that time. He became President of Princeton University in 1812, and Moderator of the General Assembly in 1824.

[244] Custis, p. 435.

[245] Meade, Vol. II, p. 248.

[246] Kirkland, p. 208.

[247] Baker: After the Revolution, p. 226.

[248] Sparks, Vol. X, p. 179.

[249] Long Island, Vol. IV, p. 311.

[250] Rush, p. 65.

[251] Meade, Vol. II, p. 494; [252] p. 494; [253] p. 492.

[254] Norton, p. 394.

[255] Sparks, Vol. X, p. 222; [256] p. 286; [257] p. 309.

[258] Sparks, Vol. X, p. 389; [259] p. 393.

[260] Baker: After the Revolution, p. 272.

[261] Long Island, Vol. IV, p. 76.

[262] Baker: After the Revolution, p. 286.

[263] Sparks, Vol. XII, p. 54; [264] pp. 132, 134.

[265] Baker: After the Revolution, p. 305.

[266] Sparks, Vol. XII, pp. 56, 60, 64; [267] pp. 227, 228.

[268] Meade, Vol. II, p. 243.

[269] Custis, p. 75.

[270] Sparks, Vol. XII, pp. 65, 74.

[271] Custis, p. 78.

[272] Green, p. 157; [273] p. 614; [274] p. 615.

[275] Baker: After the Revolution, p. 368.

[276] Eulogies and Orations, p. 258.

[277] Johnston, p. 121.

[278] Pryor, p. 351.

[279] M'Guire, p. 154; [280] p. 154.

[281] Meade, Vol. II, p. 246.

[282] Walter, p. 233.

[283] Lossing: Mary and Martha, p. 324.

[284] Sparks, Vol. I, p. 558.

[285] Weems, p. 168.

[286] M'Guire, p. 344.

[287] Weems, p. 169.

[288] Hough, Vol. I, p. 17.

[289] Weems, p. 170. Washington died between ten and eleven o'clock Saturday night, December 14, 1799, in the 68th year of his age.

[290] Sparks, Vol. I, p. 529.

[291] Custis, p. 477.

[292] Lossing: Mary and Martha, p. 327.

[293] Custis, p. 509; [294] p. 513.   Mrs. Washington died Saturday evening, May 22, 1802.

[295] Ramsay, p. 361.

[296] Ramsay, p. 358; [297] p. 352; [298] p. 353.

[299] Sparks, Vol. XII, pp. 405–407; [300] p. 407; [301] p. 407–8.

[302] Littell, p. 14.

[303] Meade, Vol. II, p. 243.

[304] Eulogies and Orations, p. 17; [305] p. 37; [306] p. 292; [307] p. 279; [308] p. 91; [309] p. 233; [310] p. 190.

[311] Baker: Character Portraits, p. 114—Timothy Dwight, D.D., President of Yale College, in Discourse on the Character of Washington, February 22, 1800.

[312] M'Guire, p. 393.

[313] Baker: Early Sketches, p. 27.

[314] Baker: Early Sketches, p. 74.

[315] Tribune, p. 7, quoted by Reverend Doctor Randolph H. McKim; [316] p. 7.

[317] Tribune, p. 7, Letter by R. C. L. Vigelius.

[318] Baker: Character Portraits, p. 284—Lecture by Theodore Parker, 1858.

[319] Kirkland, p. 480.

[320] Weems, p. 62.

[321] Bancroft (Aaron), p. 538.

[322] Edmonds, Vol. II, p. 304.

[323] Marshall, Vol. II, p. 445.

[324] Bancroft (George), Vol. VII, p. 398.

[325] Sparks, Vol. I, p. 535.

[326] Sparks, Vol. XII, p. 411.

WHERE FOUND

[327] Ramsay, p. 331.
[328] Paulding, Vol. II, p. 208; [329] p. 210.
[330] Trevelyan, Vol. III, p. 308; [331] p. 310.
[332] Lodge, Vol. II, p. 387.
[333] Weems, p. 174.

NAMES OF THE DEITY

THE terms one uses in referring to the Deity are an indication of his religious thinking, and of his conception of God and his attributes. In the quotations found in this book, Washington uses no less than fifty-four designations. In the following list are twenty-six more, which are found in his writings, but not quoted in this volume.

The page on which the name first occurs is given.

Almighty.
Almighty Being, 161.
Almighty Father, 126.
Almighty God, 81.
Almighty Ruler of the Universe, 113.
All-Kind Providence.
All-Powerful Guide, 150.
All-Powerful Providence, 47.
All-Wise Dispenser of Events, 70.
All-Wise Disposer of Events, 70.
All-Wise and Powerful Being, 111.
Author of All Good, 114.
Author of Blessings, 216.

Being, 72.
Beloved Son, 127.
Beneficent Author of All Good, 173.

NAMES OF THE DEITY

Beneficent Being.
Benign Parent of the Human Race, 162.
Bountiful Providence, 119.

Creator, 172.

Deity, 165.
Dispenser of Human Events, 150.
Divine Author of Life and Felicity, 225.
Divine Author of Our Blessed Religion, 141.
Divine Author of the Universe.
Divine Beneficence, 215.
Divine Blessing.
Divine Goodness, 113.
Divine Government, 133.
Divine Providence, 164.

Giver of Life, 227.
Giver of Victory, 81.
God, 39.
God of Armies, 144.
Good Providence, 172.
Gracious and Beneficent Being.
Gracious God.
Gracious Providence.
Grand Architect of the Universe.
Great Arbiter of the Universe.
Great Author of All the Care and Good, 114.
Great Director of Events.
Great Disposer of Events.
Great Father of the Universe.
Great and Glorious Being, 173.

Great and Good Being, 111
Great Governor of the Universe, 164.
Great Power.
Great Ruler of Events.
Great Ruler of Nations, 216.
Great Searcher of Human Hearts.

Heaven, 69.
Heavenly Preserver, 125.

Jehovah.

Kind Providence, 226.

Lord, 81.
Lord and Giver of All Victory, 77.
Lord of Hosts, 77.
Lord and Ruler of Nations, 174.

Maker.
Most Gracious Being, 158.

Omnipotent Being, 155.
Overruling Providence.

Parent of the Universe.
Power.
Providence, 39.

Revelation, Pure and Benign Light of, 140.
Ruler of the Universe, 220.

Source of Blessings.

NAMES OF THE DEITY

Sovereign Arbiter of the United States, 221.
Superintending Providence.
Supreme Architect.
Supreme Author of All Good, 112.
Supreme Being, 82.
Supreme Dispenser of Every Good.
Supreme Ruler of Nations, 214.
Supreme Ruler of the Universe, 171.

Wise Disposer of Events.
Wonder-Working Deity.

INDEX

INDEX

Canada, message to, 72

Chaplain, asks for, 45

Chaplains, commends, 138

Chapman, the Rev. George Thomas, statement by, 187

Character sketch, 120

"Charity, example of Christian," 108

Charity, to the poor, 72; gift to, 211; bequest, 240

Chatterton Hill, battle of, 84

Children, adopts, 134

Christ Church, Alexandria, Virginia; see "Alexandria, Virginia"

Christ Church, Cambridge, Massachusetts, 74

Christ Church, Philadelphia, Pennsylvania, attends, 66, 152; pew in, 191, 192, 193

Christian above patriot, 112

Christian, letter of Nelly Custis, 243

Christian soldier, 83

Christmas, poem, 21; at church, 146

Church attendance, 39, 55, 57, 62, 63, 66, 74, 120, 134, 146, 149, 150, 151, 152, 154, 155, 160, 185, 190, 191, 201, 226, 243

Church attendance at home, 153

Church attendance in Philadelphia, 190, 191

Church, attends at inauguration, 160

Church building committee, member of, Falls Church, 53; chairman, Payne's Church, 54; chairman, Pohick Church, 55

Church, Christmas at, 146

Church, goes to, 152

Church, going in family coach, 60

Church, his custom to attend, 39, 184, 194, 243

Church, not kept from by company, 56

Church, member of, 148

Church membership of parents, 18

Church of England, parents members of, 18; subscribes to doctrine and discipline, 50

Church, Falls, 53

Church, panic in, 154

Church, Payne's, 53

Church, Pohick, 54

Church, Pope's Creek, 19

Church, Saint Peter's, Kent County, Virginia, 48

Church, Saint Peter's, Philadelphia, 66, 192

Church subscriptions, 185

Church, Trumbull attends with Washington, 134

Church, Washington at, in Philadelphia, 193; in Alexandria, 228

Churchman, claimed to be, 249

Clergy, address of, 221, 222

Clergy, regard for, 139

Communicant, 55, 57, 187

Communion, partook regularly, 58; attends at Morristown, New Jersey, 85; withdraws from, 96; partakes of, 194; always before Revolution, 244

Confirmed, not, 58

Congregational Church, attends, 74, 176

Congress, speech to, 217; last speech to, 220

Conscience, rights of, 70

Constitutional convention, president of, 152

Contemplations: Moral and Divine, 19

INDEX

INDEX

INDEX

Washington, Bushrod, nephew, testimony of, 258

Washington, John, great-grandfather, 16

Washington, L a w r e n c e, grandfather, 16

Washington, L a w r e n c e, brother, 21; visits West Indies, 22; son-in-law of Mr. Fairfax, 38

Washington, Lund, business agent, 73

Washington, Mary B a l l, mother, 17

Washington, Martha, wife, married, 48; always sympathized with husband, 67; letters to, 68; asks church be prepared for services, 75; attends church at Cambridge, 75; at son's death; 135; goes to New York, 162; attends consecration of Trinity Church, 182; in prayer, 234; at husband's deathbed, 235; daily devotions, 235; death, 236; very pious, 243–245.

Washington, the Rev. Lawrence, great-great-grandfather, 16

Wellington, Duke of, quoted, 269

West Indies, trip to, 22

"Whiskey Rebellion," 214

W h i t e, Bishop William, preaches, 152; statement of, 191, 193, 196; letter, 246

Wife, letters to, 68

Will, Washington's, 237

Winthrop, Robert C., testimony of, 257

Wylie, the Rev. T. W. J., testimony of, 105

RECOMMENDED FURTHER READING

If you liked this book, the editors of Mott Media suggest that you order one or more of the following biographies of famous Christians.

ABRAHAM LINCOLN THE CHRISTIAN
This book answers the questions which have surrounded the sincerity of Lincoln's spiritual life. The author demonstrates that the president moved through several stages of religious activity until a family tragedy caused him to give his life to Christ.

ROBERT E. LEE THE CHRISTIAN
Robert E. Lee is revealed as a deeply religious man who sought God's will in the decisions which were forced upon him. Throughout the turmoil of conflict, he remained consistent to his God and Saviour. His true Christian character presents a challenge to every believer today.

FOR YOUNG READERS AGES 8-12

ISAAC NEWTON
John Tiner's biography of Isaac Newton fills a gap in our knowledge and understanding of the spiritual life of a man who is usually recognized only for his scientific achievements. His inventions have overshadowed his lifelong practice of Bible study and prayer.

For more information on the above books: Write:

MOTT MEDIA, P.O. Box 236, MILFORD, MI 48042

NAME _____

ADDRESS _____

CITY _____ STATE _____ ZIP _____

SELECTION(S) _____

_____